# INTERNATIONAL INDUSTRY ACCLAIM FOR:
## How to get a mentor as a designer, guaranteed

*"If you want a career as a creative pro, it's not just about hard work. Finding the right mentor is key. Their guidance can save you years of struggle and give you a massive advantage. Ram's book 'How to get a mentor as a designer, guaranteed' is far and away the single best resource I've seen on the topic. It's not if you will buy this book … it's when."*

— **Chase Jarvis,** *Founder and CEO, CreativeLive*

*"Mentorship is an essential part of growing as a designer – and, really, as a human being – but it's not a topic that's well covered within design circles. Ram's book breaks this down in a way that is approachable for anyone, whether they're starting out in their career, developing further, or looking to become a mentor to others. He also does a fantastic job of describing exactly what makes mentorship important – establishing a reciprocal relationship in which both mentor and mentee learn from each other in a culture of respect, reflection and general interest in a fellow person."*

— **Ben Fullerton,** *Design Director, Nike+*

*"Ram's book provides a deeply thoughtful and practical step-by-step guide to craft your character as a designer. It's a powerful resource that addresses a wide range of readers from design students to design professionals. The best part of this book is that his guidance becomes a personalised mentoring experience for you – compelling you to act immediately."*

— **Kevin Lee,** *Global Head of Design, VISA*

*"Reading through Ram's masterful advice and guidance is a reminder that one should always be in search of mentors – no matter what stage of career or life we find ourselves in. This book will be on my shelf as a gentle nudge that I will never be done learning from others and growing as a designer."*

— Nelson Kunkel, **National Creative Director, Deloitte Digital**

*"Designers, take note; the greatest weapon against mediocrity and drifting blindly is mentorship. In this book, Ram has created an easy to follow guide to getting a mentor that aligns with your values and goals. I highly recommend it to anyone struggling to navigate today's fast-moving, professional landscape."*

— Chris Maclean, **Creative Director, RE**

*"Wish I had this book when I started my design path; hell, wish I had this when I was 12! Structured wonderfully in easy bite-sized and coherent chunks, this book will be so valuable to anyone looking to improve their design career. Mentors have been the cornerstone of my development as a professional, and as a fully rounded human. Starting with my teachers, and then peers, and now business leaders and world-class creatives, without them I wouldn't be the man I am today."*

— JP Stallard, **Co-founder at SOLV
and Samsung UK's first Interaction Designer**

*"Having a mentor is a must. Since the very beginning of my business, I've sought the help of mentors. In this simple, yet powerful book, Ram shows you the way to find and get the most out of a mentor. Great read!"*

— Jules Marcoux, **#1 best-selling author on Amazon
of The Marketing Blueprint**

*"If you want to level up your career you MUST get a mentor – and Ram Castillo is the perfect guide for this journey. In his latest book, How to get a mentor as a designer, guaranteed, designers and creatives will find a step-by-step, heart-centered process for approaching, learning from and building real relationships with mentors. This is a must-read for people looking for something more in their career."*

**– Vanessa Van Edwards,** *Behavioural Investigator, ScienceofPeople.com*

*"Where was Ram when I was emerging as a designer? This truly is a unique resource that cuts through the bullshit, with clear-cut steps on how to get the mentor who's right for you. Guaranteed."*

**– Jacob Cass,** *Founder, JUST Creative*

*"Imagine being handed a guidebook that guaranteed time travel. It is likely you would pay nearly anything for it! This book is that guide. Mentoring is the time travel. In a moment, you can learn something that might otherwise take years or decades to learn that then propels you years ahead. Ram gifts the world with the most comprehensive guide on mentoring that I have seen. If you don't have a mentor, get this book at all costs!"*

**– Daniel Flynn,** *MD and Co-founder of Thankyou, best selling author of 'Chapter One', a world first book*

*"Often young people are too timid to contact mentors or feel they don't have enough experience to make the approach. Anything that can remove that fear – like this book – is a good thing. Miss out on mentoring and you could be missing out on one of the biggest learning supports of your lifetime."*

— Andrew Hoyne, *Founder and Creative Director, Hoyne (Melbourne, Sydney & Brisbane)*

*"Ram's series of books are giving young creatives today a shortcut to a successful path. Navigating the creative industry can be a lonely journey. Like any great adventure, there's pitfalls and challenges, which can slow you down and cast doubt. How to get a mentor as a designer, guaranteed is the perfect instruction manual to find your compass in preparation for your journey."*

— Declan Mimnagh, *Senior Manager, Creative and Production, Expedia*

*"Even after six years working as a graphic designer, I find Ram's guide incredibly useful. It is not only for those starting out, but for anyone willing to learn from people they admire. I thank Ram for his generosity and passion in helping, sharing and pushing us to explore our potential."*

— Danling Xiao, *Founder, Mundane Matters*

*"If you have a real passion for design, when you find someone who still has a similar passion after years as a practising designer you will have found your mentor. By tapping into your mentor's wisdom you will 'turbo charge' your design career. If you are considering this book, you are on your way to finding your 'turbocharger' and thus fulfilling your passion for design."*

— Robyn Wakefield, *Managing Director, Walterwakefield*

*"WOW and WOW, this is one powerful book. Having mentors has been paramount to achieving success in all areas of my life. From a successful career at the world's most innovative company Salesforce.com, to becoming an Australian champion fitness model: Mr Physique Australia, an international speaker and landing numerous magazine covers, all while launching a global online coaching platform and top selling supplement brand.*

*None of this would have been possible without having mentors. I wish I had read this book 5 years ago! I felt empowered after reading it to raise my standards and live an extraordinary life."*

– **Ben "AbStacker" Handsaker,** *Founder of Abstacker.com, Australian Fitness Model, Musclemania Physique Pro and International Speaker*

# HOW TO GET A MENTOR AS A DESIGNER, GUARANTEED

---

THE 12-STEP GUIDE FOR EMERGING
AND ESTABLISHED DESIGNERS

---

**RAM CASTILLO**

Published in Australia by Ram Castillo, 2016

Cover and book design by Ram Castillo

Editor: Fiona Sim, Salamander Productions

Typesetting and publishing assistance by Publicious
www.publicious.com.au

For general information or enquiries, please contact Ram Castillo via email:
ram@giantthinkers.com

More information can be found on:
www.gettingamentor.com and www.giantthinkers.com

Copyright © Ram Castillo 2016

ISBN: 978-0-9925700-2-6 (pbk)
ISBN: 978-0-9925700-3-3 (ebk)

All rights reserved. No part of this publication may be reproduced, distributed, or transmitted in any form or by any means, including photocopying, recording, or other electronic or mechanical methods, without the prior written permission of the author.

By entering this book, readers acknowledge, understand and agree that the guarantee (stated in the book title) is subject to their ability to execute all the information in this book and the response of a mentor. As with any mentorship, it requires a certain level of competence and a demonstrated understanding of the responsibilities set by the required criteria of a mentor. The author can take no responsibility for the mentorship outcome for the readers of this book since the outcome depends on the readers' actions and other factors outside of the author's control. This includes but is not limited to, time, money, personal circumstances and mentor discretion.

While the author has used his best efforts in preparing this book, he makes no representations or warranties with respect to the accuracy or completeness of the contents of the book and specifically disclaims any implied warranties for a particular purpose. The advice and strategies contained herein may not be suitable for your situation. You should consult with a professional where appropriate.

The author shall not be liable for damages arising from this book. If the reader has executed everything recommended in this book and has still been unsuccessful after numerous attempts to find a mentor, they may be considered for a full refund of the purchase price of the book subject to providing satisfactory evidence of their outcome. This includes (but is not limited to) documented evidence of the activities and exercises completed as instructed in chapters1 to 9, and written conversation trails as advised in chapters 10 to 12. These are some of the documentary evidence required to assess whether the reader has executed the entire content of this book in order for consideration of a full refund to occur.

TO SALVE REGINA,
WHO TAUGHT ME
THAT THERE IS STILL
TIME TO CHANGE
THE ROAD YOU'RE ON.
WHATEVER THAT
ROAD MAY BE.

## MY NAME IS

_____

## I NEED A MENTOR BECAUSE

_____

_____

_____

_____

_____

_____

*Estimated section reading time: 2 minutes*

# FOREWORD

I've been blessed throughout my career to have had some of the best mentors in the business – Ted Horton, Bob Isherwood, Tom McFarlane, Maurice Saatchi, Bob Scarpelli, Keith Reinhard – to name a few. Each of them made me a better creative and, eventually, a better leader. My first mentor, and first boss, Gordon Dawson, helped me understand what it takes to be a proper writer. In my first week on the job he asked me if I'd read *Catch 22, Slaughterhouse Five, Brave New World* and about a dozen other novels. Of course, I'd read almost none of them. So he bought me a huge stack of paperbacks and told me to start reading. There's no doubt that he made me better. And it's a lesson that has stuck with me my entire life.

Keith Reinhard, Chairman Emeritus at DDB and lifelong mentor, once said of my role as a Chief Creative Officer, "Your job is not to create great advertising. It's to cause it." That's become a mantra for me. In many cases, the advice I have received from mentors has literally changed the trajectory of my career. That's why this book is so important.

Further, the beauty of this book is that the author is not some high-flying exec, long detached from the reality of working life. Ram Castillo writes this book from the trenches. From the point of view of a working designer who is always trying to improve his skills. From the point of view of someone who, himself, actively seeks mentorship. In fact, that's how Ram and I first met; some years ago he interviewed me for his blog about advice for young creatives trying to break into the industry.

Ram is on a mission to make the industry better, not just for designers but for all creatives. Having a mentor will not only make you better, it will make the industry better. It's as simple as that.

In this, his second book, Ram jumps straight from the theoretical to the practical. This is not just a book about making a plan, this is a book about taking action. Nelson Mandela once said, "There is no passion to be found in playing small – in settling for a life that is less than the one you are capable of living." Ram has laid out, in simple terms, the steps it will take to live the (professional) life you are capable of living.

**Matt Eastwood,**
Worldwide Chief Creative Officer
J. Walter Thompson
*New York, 29 July 2016*

# CONTENTS

| | |
|---|---|
| INTRODUCTION | 1 |
| MY INVITATION TO YOU | 6 |
| WHO THIS BOOK IS FOR | 10 |
| WHAT IS A MENTOR? | 16 |
| WHAT IS A MENTEE? | 18 |
| WHAT IS MENTORSHIP? | 21 |
| HOW A SIDE STEP CAN LEAD TO A FORWARD STEP | 26 |
| EXPOSURE AND CONDITIONING | 32 |
| THREE LESSONS FROM MY MOST INFLUENTIAL CAREER MENTOR | 34 |
| LONG FOR 'BETTER' | 42 |
| THE 12 KEY STEPS TO MENTORSHIP | 50 |
| THREE POINTS TO KEEP IN MIND | 164 |
| PARTING WORDS | 172 |
| ACKNOWLEDGEMENTS | 180 |
| RECOMMENDED RESOURCES | 183 |
| INDEX | 188 |

# A SMALL STEP IN THE RIGHT DIRECTION TRUMPS A BIG STEP IN THE WRONG ONE.

— RAM CASTILLO

*Estimated chapter reading time: 5 minutes*

# INTRODUCTION

## HERE ARE THE FIVE MAIN LESSONS YOU'LL WALK AWAY WITH FROM THIS BOOK:

- You will better understand why you need a mentor.
- You will be able to cultivate your value offering to prospective mentors.
- You will know how to gather then curate the specific mentors in line with your goals.
- You will learn how to approach, make contact with and create rapport with your listed prospects.
- You will be able to navigate your way in the mentor–mentee relationship.

**If these ideas resonate with you, I invite you to keep reading.**

# WHY YOU NEED TO READ THIS BOOK

**You deserve to succeed faster
and be fulfilled deeper.**

Whether you agree with this statement or not,
I certainly believe you do. Why? Why not.

And I use the terms 'succeed' and 'fulfilled'
in accordance with your personal definition
of those words.

I've written this for emerging and established
designers who want success and fulfilment,
although most principles presented in this book
are transferrable and applicable to non-design
related industries too.

Regardless of industry, most people are taking
the long route to their professional and personal
development goals. I certainly did in patches and
waves. We can often be overwhelmed. Do the wrong
things in the wrong order. Burn time and energy
re-inventing the wheel.

If you are indeed a designer, as the title suggests (emerging or established), you must continually cast a wider net in character development. Growth, maturity and understanding in business, leadership, ethics, economics, empathy and relationships are just a few dimensions that require constant nurturing.

If you truly believe that being a designer is more than a title that sits under your name on LinkedIn, then I have no doubt you believe in the necessity of being mentored.

Furthermore, being a designer is more than crafting or executing. It's a process of unravelling human-centred problems while considering intentions, organisational objectives and future ecosystems. This 'process' is a constant tango of discovery, which demands that the designer participate in multi-layered conversations. So, our ability to problem solve is directly in proportion to our experiences. This includes the depth and breadth of our interactions, and the quality of our relationships.

For this very reason, many designers understand the importance of getting a mentor, but just don't know how to go about it. If this sounds like you, then you're in the right place to bridge that gap.

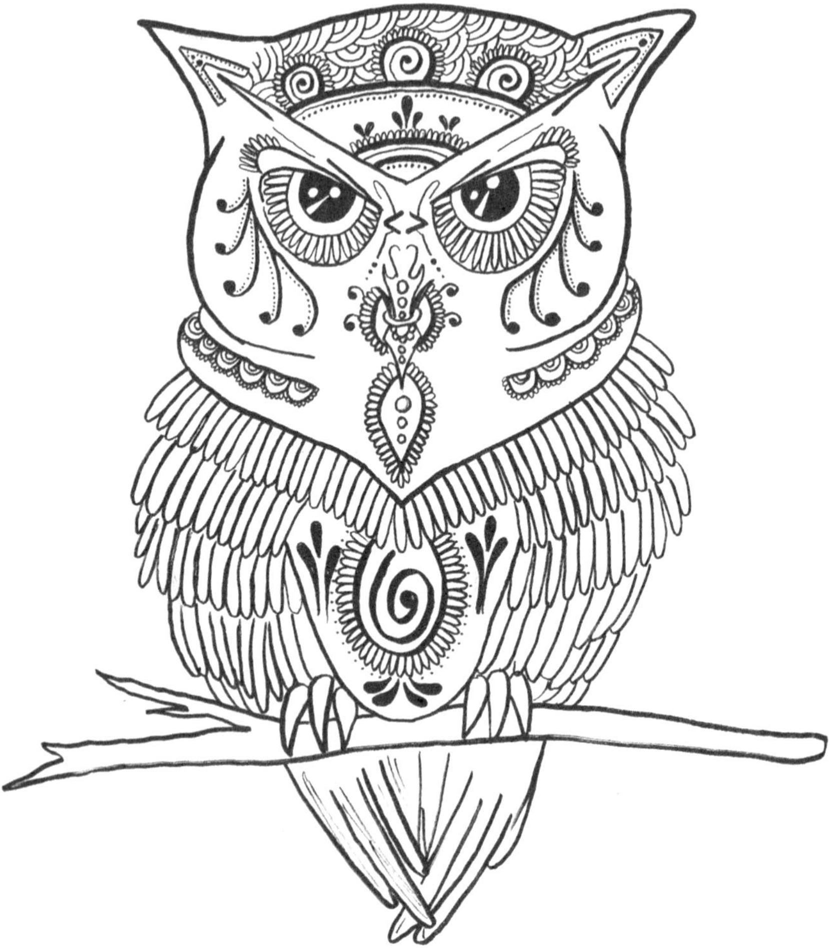

HAVING A MENTOR GIVES ME INSIGHTS INTO THINGS I WOULDN'T OTHERWISE SEE IN THE DARK.

— KRISHIA CATABAY,
@THECBAYS

*Estimated chapter reading time: 5 minutes*

# MY INVITATION TO YOU

Writing this at 30 years of age, I suspect that to some degree (even subconsciously) we have many similarities. I make this assumption because if you've been drawn to this book, it means that you're searching deeply for guidance. I too felt this 10, 15, even 20 years ago.

I lacked self-belief, self-confidence and direction. For me, this translated to the fact that I was shy, short and a Filipino immigrant from a low- to middle-income family. I was never the smartest, never the fittest, always the shortest and never the most popular.

All of these attributes were reflected in my pile of participation awards (at best, third place ribbons), the fact that I was always selected for the B-grade squad of every team sport I trialled for and only broke into circles of the female species by lathering myself up daily with the scent of 'friend zone'. And on days where I felt I started to make some ground, my crooked teeth, acne and middle-child syndrome jumped in to pull me back down.

Little did I realise, that despite all this, I had won the geographical lottery; being raised in Sydney, Australia – a first-world country. Everything I wanted to change, improve on and be better at was within arm's reach. All I needed to do was ask the right questions to the right people. Who knew? In school, I certainly didn't.

Between then and now, I've cracked a code that has worked for me and my peers. I have absolute confidence that it will work for you too. It's fast-tracked me to a life as a design director, author, blogger, top-ranking podcaster and speaker by the age of 30. A lifestyle that has led me to be featured in *HOW* and *Communication Arts* magazines and AIGA, the professional association for design. It's led me to speak at Apple, CreativeLive and Herman Miller. As well as this, I've been able to interview some of the brightest minds in our industry including global head of design for VISA, Kevin Lee; global chief creative officer for JWT, Matt Eastwood and design director for Nike+, Ben Fullerton. This journey has stamped more than 100 cities in over 30 countries on my passport.

Now reading that back, I'm fully aware that I risk sounding egotistical and self-absorbed. However, know that I mean well. And in order for me to fully gain your trust and attention, I must paint a picture of some level of credibility. Nothing makes me hit the close button faster than someone presenting an idea without sufficient research, well-rounded information and above all, proven personal experience.

**So, I'm going to introduce to you my perspective, to share with you my methodology and worldview on how to get a mentor as a designer.**

This doesn't mean my way is the only way, as there's always more than one way of doing anything. Anyone who tells you that their way is the only way is lying to you. We are all complex and unique human beings with different gifts, personalities and experiences.

Finding a mentor may be confronting. You may need to change your current approach and way of working. This applies to people who feel they're already successful too. For instance, if one was to say "I've already made a million dollars", the other perspective is that this is a failed business because it has not made five million dollars.

Speaking of millions, there are millions of doors that are presented to us in our lifetime. Hundreds daily. The question is, are you going to step through this one? The truth is, I believe you're going to get 'there' regardless. But do you want to get there quicker? This is the opportunity I'm presenting to you.

When I asked the thousands of emerging and established designers on my mailing list the question "What is it that you need that you feel I can give you?", hundreds replied within 24 hours saying that they wanted a mentor. Perhaps this response was partly elicited by the screaming truth and realisation of the saying "You are the average of the five people you hang around".

I'm also predicting that if you've picked up this book, you've realised that if you don't prioritise your own life, someone else will. The pain point here is that we all know time is not a renewable resource.

So if we acknowledge how powerful mentorship is in helping us produce the results we're after, why do most of us only have one or two mentors in our lives, such as our parents or teachers (likely due to situation or circumstance such as proximity), or maybe none at all?

*Estimated chapter reading time: 5 minutes*

# WHO THIS BOOK IS FOR

## HAVE YOU EVER FELT THESE COMMON BARRIERS TO MENTORSHIP?

- I don't know where to start
- I don't know where to look
- I don't have any contacts
- I don't know what to say to a prospective mentor
- I don't know what's an acceptable arrangement
- I don't have the confidence.

**If you have, take comfort in knowing that the answers are in this book.**

Let me tell you, I can completely empathise with those frustrations. It's bloody hard! I mean, they didn't exactly teach us how to open a conversation in school. Not just with potential employers or clients, but with anyone.

We weren't told about tone of voice or how to build rapport. We weren't taught about how to make a good first impression or what we can leverage to make it a win-win situation. Heck, if it wasn't for reality TV, we wouldn't even know the importance of eye contact, posture and to smile, as we cringe at the bombardment of poor interactions, showing us clearly what not to do.

We eventually just pick up rapport building through trial and error, and observation. So then what? Are these the only tools we must continue to use and rely on for creating and developing quality connections? Surely not.

In this book, I'm going to close that information gap.

**I will guide you on how get a mentor in 12 steps.**

For the record, to punch your demons in the face, here's a quick hit of fire power against those common barriers:

- *I don't know where to start.*
  **You've already started.**
- *I don't know where to look.*
  **They're definitely on planet earth.**
- *I don't have any contacts.*
  **We'll work on meeting new people.**
- *I don't know what to say to a prospective mentor.*
  **It's in doing, that you'll find the words.**
- *I don't know what's an acceptable arrangement.*
  **Neither did they when they stood where you're standing.**
- *I don't have the confidence.*
  **You will, when you uncover your worth through exposure and conditioning.**

Let's look at your perceived barriers as what they are, not worse than they are.

Not being able to buy a $3.50 latte every single day doesn't make you poor. Nor does lack of knowledge in a particular subject make you dumb. You get the idea.

**WE ARE DROWNING IN INFORMATION, WHILE STARVING FOR WISDOM.**

— E. O. WILSON

# MY INTENTION FOR YOU

Firstly, I want you to feel like you're not alone.

Secondly, I want to break down any fear and intimidation you may have towards prospective mentors.

Thirdly, the success of this book will be measured by more than what is written on the cover. I have no doubt you'll get a mentor (or ten) by taking in and utilising the steps in this book.

**The true measure is walking away with:**

- clarity
- a firm conviction of feeling grounded
- an increase of curiosity
- an expansion of vision
- a heightening of self-awareness
- a deepened sensitivity to authentic human connection.

> **A TRUE MENTOR WILL TRY TO LIFT OTHER PEOPLE UP ABOVE THEM.**
>
> — RAM CASTILLO

*Estimated chapter reading time: 1 minute*

# WHAT IS A MENTOR?

A mentor is someone who constructively guides, actively participates in supportive dialogue, and becomes a role model to a person less experienced than they are, particularly in the area of professional or personal development.

## MY FRAMEWORK FOR THE THREE PILLARS OF A MENTOR:

- Guidance (advises, recommends and supervises constructively – similar to a coach).

- Support (listens, counsels, encourages, inspires and motivates – similar to a friend).

- Role model (practices what they preach through their actions – similar to an idol).

Three pillars of a mentor diagram

**GUIDANCE**
COACH

**SUPPORT**
FRIEND

**ROLE MODEL**
IDOL

*Estimated chapter reading time: 1 minute*

# WHAT IS A MENTEE?

A mentee is a person who is advised, trained or counselled by a mentor.

## MY FRAMEWORK FOR THE THREE PILLARS OF A MENTEE:

- Willingness (to try, to be open minded, to explore – a decision of the mind).
- Action (to follow through, to move, to plant seeds – a decision of the body).
- Commitment (to persevere, to be resilient, to push through barriers – a decision of the spirit).

Three pillars of a mentee diagram

**WILLINGNESS**
MIND

**ACTION**
BODY

**COMMITMENT**
SPIRIT

—

# I'VE BEEN A MENTEE MY ENTIRE LIFE AND I WILL BE A MENTEE FOR THE REST OF IT.

— RAM CASTILLO

—

*Estimated chapter reading time: 5 minutes*

# WHAT IS MENTORSHIP?

Mentorship in its complete sense is a two-way street. It is in reflective, collaborative, back-and-forth conversations that learning outcomes are achieved, assessed and measured as legitimate progress.

Don't get me wrong, reading a book, listening to a podcast interview or completing a video course from someone whose footsteps you'd like to follow in are all brilliant. However, for the sake of a clear definition, as you can see in the three pillars of a mentor, this person you admire only becomes a coach and an idol. This certainly is not to dismiss the massive value this type of relationship provides. It simply means the support and constructive sounding board of a friend isn't there.

# WHAT MAKES US CRAVE A MENTOR?

Now… the problem is this…

How do we get from where we are now to where we want to be?

Navigating our way to our end goals can sometimes leave us feeling lost, disappointed and drained. But there is a way to lessen the wrong turns and that's what you'll be walking away with by reading this book.

**EVERYTHING WE HAVE RIGHT NOW BEGAN WITH NOTHING BUT A THOUGHT. AN IDEA IN OUR MINDS.**

— RAM CASTILLO

Are you particularly happy with something you've achieved? This might be an aspect of your career, a learnt skill set, a financial milestone, or a health and fitness goal.

All those good things started with a deliberate and intentional decision within yourself, didn't they?

But here's the all-important part two of this process: "What got you here won't get you there".

In order to elevate your thoughts and actions, and fast track your progress, you need to be informed by experts in your particular space of interest.

**By getting a mentor, you cut the guesswork and decisions that are costing you lost time, money and effort. A mentor can show you the shortcuts, help you see the blind spots and help you succeed faster.**

When you look at experts you admire, do you ever wonder who are they, really? I mean, how on earth did they get to that level?

From a distance, it's easy to assume that a mentor is more intelligent, more fearless and gifted than you in your current state. However, it's not that at all. It's just that they've played that game before, over and over again.

The fear, the anxiety, the challenges, the unknown, are and will always be there. This is because the stakes will continue to get higher and you'll have more to lose. Such as more wealth and equity in your brand, credibility, network quality and financial assets.

The big difference is that over time, you'll simply learn how to manage those emotions better.

*Estimated chapter reading time: 10 minutes*

# HOW A SIDE STEP CAN LEAD TO A FORWARD STEP

Before we dive into the juicy practicalities in this book, I'll briefly share with you a few key events that may influence your decisions moving forward.

It may widen your version of what you think of as a 'right' or 'wrong' professional development decision.

What's come to surface in my life over time is that seemingly unrelated experiences from the past can actually prepare us perfectly for our sought-after destination.

When I started high school, I had already decided that when I finished I wanted to be employed as a graphic designer. How that was going to unfold was a puzzle.

All I knew was that in Australia, the legal minimum age to work was 14 years and 9 months. So my plan was to work anywhere to demonstrate that I was employable in the first place. A tiny part of that journey, and what I learnt, looked like this:

## I WAS A CHECKOUT OPERATOR

**Age: 14 years and 9 months**
Employed at: Woolworths (large grocery chain)

*What I learnt most:*

- how to make eye contact, smile and say hello fluidly (in that order) – i.e. body language
- to be conscious of tone, rhythm, pace and volume in my voice when communicating with customers
- resolving customer disputes
- punctuality
- confidence
- the starting baseline of a personal income
- cash handling and payment systems.

# I WAS A SERVICE ATTENDANT

**Age: 16 years**

Employed at: Something Fruity
(premium health food store)

*What I learnt most:*

- portion control
- opening and closing a shop
- accountability.

# I WAS A MEMBER OF THE FLOOR STAFF

**Age: 17 years**

Employed at: KMART and Surf Dive 'n' Ski

*What I learnt most:*

- inventory
- product categories
- presentation affects sales.

## I WAS A GLASS COLLECTOR THEN BARTENDER

**Age: 18 years**

Employed at: Establishment Bar

*What I learnt most:*

- people desire moments of escape from everyday reality
- social dynamics.


## I WAS A MAILROOM BOY

**Age: 19 years**

Employed at: Singleton Ogilvy & Mather

*What I learnt most:*

- the significance of 350 different roles in steering a large company
- process and protocol
- networking
- advertising.

# HOW ALL THIS PREPARED ME AS A DESIGNER

*Being a checkout operator:*
**To treat customers with empathy and care.**

*Being a service attendant:*
**To price products relative to their quality.**

*Being part of the floor staff:*
**Product presentation matters and inventory requires constant monitoring.**

*Being a glass collector then bartender:*
**An insight into human interactions, emotional exchanges and behavioural psychology.**

*Being a mailroom boy:*
**The mechanics of running a business and how to build a professional network.**

THE HERO
AND THE COWARD
BOTH FEEL THE SAME
THING – FEAR;
BUT IT'S WHAT
YOU DO WITH IT
THAT MATTERS.

– CONSTANTINE 'CUS' D'AMATO

*Estimated chapter reading time: 3 minutes*

# EXPOSURE AND CONDITIONING

As hinted in the beginning of this book, I never had much luck with seduction or attraction in high school. I know, I know… I can almost hear your screams of outrage! In all seriousness though, I really struggled with self-confidence and I simply did not know how to meet women.

Then one day in mid 2004, I watched a movie that you may have seen yourself, titled Troy. It starred Brad Pitt as Achilles, Diane Kruger, Eric Bana, Orlando Bloom and Rose Byrne. The movie portrays the battle between the ancient kingdoms of Troy and Sparta.

Brad Pitt was basically as shredded as a cheese grater (bear with me, this is getting somewhere!). It made me ponder the question of why male strippers are rarely ever nervous around women. Well, it's just another day in the office for them. They've exposed themselves (excuse the pun) to a level which informs them of what to expect.

This is no different to building rapport (online and offline) with key influencers, decision makers, experts and prospective mentors. Exposing yourself to opportunities to learn from others and the conditioning to deal with diverse situations will get easier the more you do it.

One big, big point I need to highlight here is the step before this, which is: being prepared.

Think back to the times that you have spoken in front of an audience; whether in school or at some type of public gathering. You would've noticed that your nervousness was directly in proportion to how prepared you were to deliver the content. The more you planned, practised and primed yourself for the task, the more ready you were to slam dunk it.

*Estimated chapter reading time: 10 minutes*

# THREE LESSONS FROM MY MOST INFLUENTIAL CAREER MENTOR

If you read my first book on how to get a job as a designer, you would remember that I mentioned a gentleman named Ian Wingrove. Allow me to expand on the story of the man who gave me a chance when no-one else did.

Over the course of a decade, Ian gently moulded me. Perhaps at times he did so unknowingly, as I observed his actions matching his words time and time again.

He taught me how to design with purpose. He taught not by ever telling me what to do, but rather, he invited me to really think about solutions on my own. He would hint, and at times suggest, and if ever I made progress, we would discuss why my solution worked. It was a bonus that, as my mentor, Ian exposed me to the idea of lifestyle design and strengthened my existing understanding of ethics (which was originally passed down from my parents).

# 1. A LESSON IN PERSISTENCE

Ian and I first met in 2001. I was 15 and in grade 10 in high school. Part of our curriculum was to explore career paths. We had to organise our own two-week work experience placement.

I literally rang 99 design companies under the 'Graphic Design Services' category of the White Pages. (If you were born after the mid-90s, you may not know this as the printed version, since they started to get phased out around that time! It was essentially a very thick phone directory of businesses around Australia – now only existing online.)

On my last day of trying to find work experience, I had my tail between my legs as I walked into the careers advisor's office. I disappointedly had to update him that of the 99 design companies I had rung, all of them had rejected me.

He then said, "Try one more". Feeling defeated, and convincing myself that I had exhausted all options, I groaned an "okay". Since the listings were in alphabetical order, I had given up on the batch below the letter 'V'. My careers advisor slid the White Pages across the table to me, and I proceeded to randomly select a design company under the letter 'W'.

"Hello, good afternoon, this is Wingrove Design", answered the receptionist. "Oh hi ... Um, I'm from Parramatta Marist High School, my name's Ram Castillo. Our school has asked all grade 10 students to organise our own two-week work experience, which is why I'm calling..." I replied. "Sure thing, can I put you on hold?" she said. "Of course" I responded, with a forced tone of enthusiasm.

"Hello, this is Ian Wingrove", said the voice of a very confident and down-to-earth man. I responded with "Ahh ... hi Ian, my name's Ram Castillo and I was wondering if you by any chance took in students for volunteer work experience? I'm currently in grade 10 and looking to know more about the design industry."

Ian replied, "We've actually never taken on high school students in the past, as our priority is to accommodate university interns. However, I appreciate the initiative, and we do have capacity. When can you start?"

"Next week if that's okay?", I replied. "No worries, see you on Monday at 9 am at the studio here in Surry Hills", said Ian.

So Monday comes and I'm as nervous as a cat crossing a street in Vietnam. The eager beaver inside me gets me there 20 minutes early. I sit on a couch in the waiting area, flicking through beautiful matte finish coffee table books on exhibition designs, typography and photography.

At around 9:10 am, a surfer-built, young and energetic looking man with Thor-like-locks, wearing a white T-shirt and cargo pants enters. He drops his skateboard on the timber floor, starts skating around for a few seconds, kicks his board up, walks towards me, extends his right hand while smiling and says, "Hey you must be Ram! I'm Ian – it's great to have you join us."

Naturally, my brain exploded. In that moment, and in the two weeks that followed, I got the warm fuzzies. This was it. I wanted to be a designer.

# 2. A LESSON IN PATIENCE

Every year thereafter, I would send Ian one or two emails to keep in touch. Usually they were "hi and hello" mid-year emails or end-of-year "Merry Christmas and Happy New Year" emails.

In 2007, at 21 years old, I got a phone call from a new number while at the gym.

"Hello, Ram speaking", I answered. "G'day Ram, it's Ian Wingrove! How are you mate?"

"Hey Ian! Wow it's been ages! I'm doing well … in between jobs at the moment, but kicking on", I responded. "Good timing", Ian said. "Before you make any decisions, I'd love to catch up. I've just started a new agency. We're pitching for a big client and could use your help."

The following day, I met Ian at his new office. I hadn't seen him in the flesh for six whole years. A lot had happened during that time. Notably, I finished design college and had an entry-level portfolio to show. Cringe-worthy to look at now! But enough for Ian to see potential.

I helped out for the week. We pitched against five other shortlisted agencies, and won.

He immediately offered me a job. My heart sang. I said "HELL YES!"

From then on, I stayed on board under Ian's guidance as a full-time designer for three years.

# 3. A LESSON IN POSSIBILITY

I have Ian to thank for awakening in me the desire to try and the permission to fail. Without Ian, this book would not exist, which for me would be a personal tragedy as I would have missed the enrichment of mentoring others myself. I thank Ian for caring enough to lead from the front, and for sharing his wisdom with me.

My hope for you reading this, is that you plant many seeds and nurture them with persistence, patience and possibility.

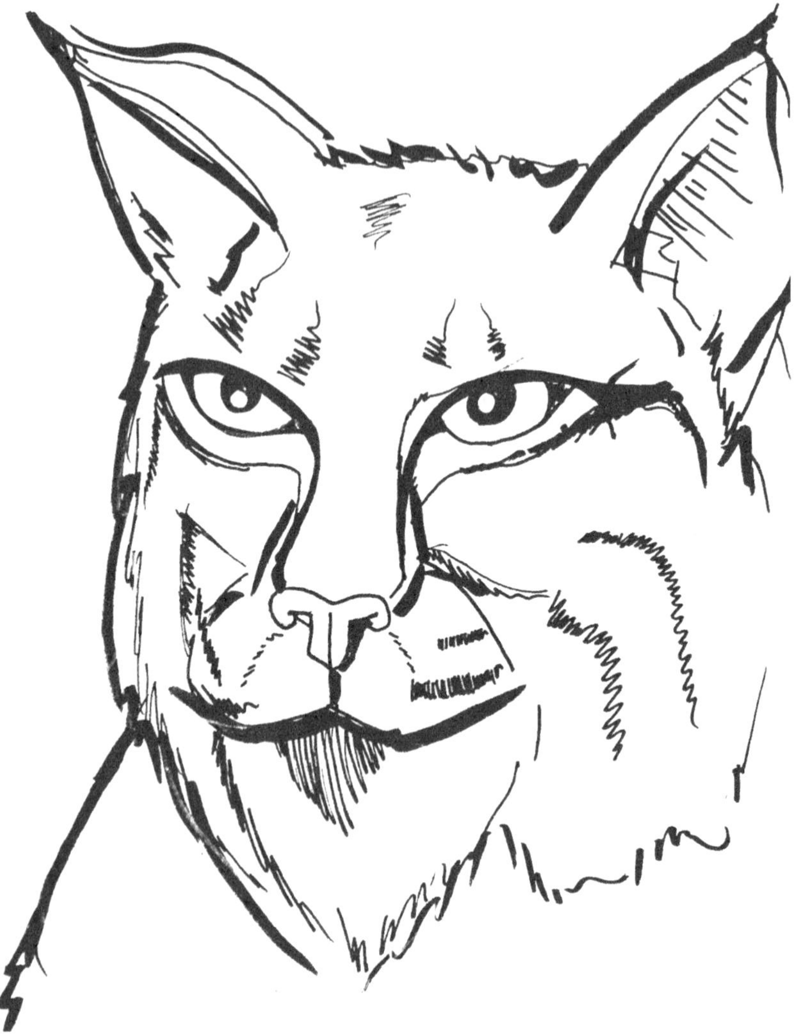

# HAVING A MENTOR WILL CREATE MINDFULNESS ALONG WITH THE ABILITY TO EXPLORE UNCHARTED TERRITORY.

— AMBROSIA SULLIVAN,
SHOE DESIGNER & ARTIST,
@DANCEDOSIADANCE

*Estimated chapter reading time: 10 minutes*

# LONG FOR 'BETTER'

The same values and qualities that I found in Ian are what draws me to other stand-out individuals. I'm sure that you can relate to this with the people you've met on your journey.

There's a quote that I really love which ties back to all of this. And that is: "If you want to be a millionaire, speak to a billionaire".

This vehicle, known as 'mentorship' is something that I have found and continually find as the common denominator for accelerating results.

It is the solution to turning this:

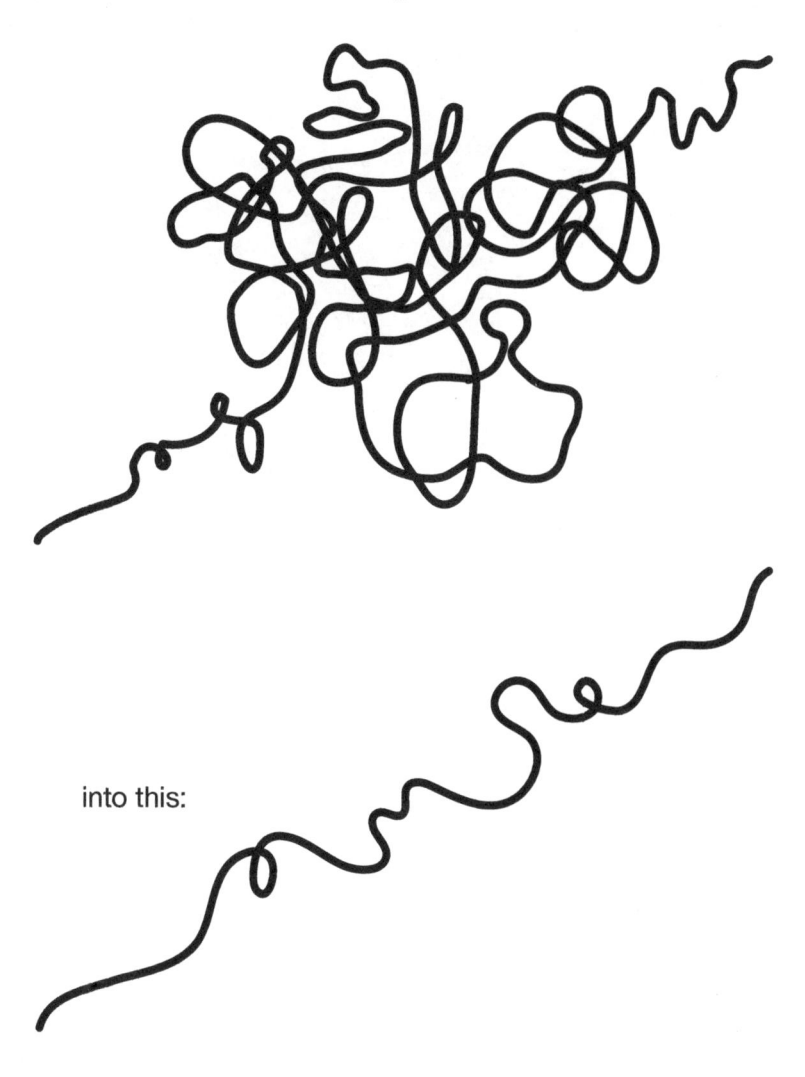

into this:

**The purpose of a mentor is to help guide your learning. Mentors have made many of the mistakes for you.**

# CALM WATERS MAKE POOR SAILORS.

— OLD PROVERB

When you think about it, if someone's doing something that you ultimately want to be doing and this person is at the top of their game in that area of expertise that you'd like to learn from, it's highly unlikely that this has happened overnight. They would've survived many storms.

**You may be familiar with the saying that "It takes ten years to be an overnight success".**

These successful people, praised in public, have spent years and years practising their craft in private. Sometimes we can forget that.

There are experts out there who are exceptional at what they do and can consistently deliver. Why is that? Well, I can tell you that it's not because they got lucky. It wasn't by chance or by accident. They've performed repetition above and beyond uncomfortable to a place on the edge of uncertainty.

—

**BE CONSTANTLY IN A STATE OF SHITTING YOURSELF.**

– DAVID 'MEGGS' HOOKE,
STREET / FINE ARTIST

—

# A COACH VERSUS A MENTOR

I should also point out that there's a difference between an instructor or coach and a mentor. A mentor embodies values and characteristics that you would like to emulate, on top of the self-improvement factor or skill set learning.

**Here are two examples:**

A personal trainer who helps you with resistance training a couple sessions a week versus a personal trainer who does that plus lives a healthy lifestyle, has a thriving small business and perhaps volunteers once a week at the local school. I'll share a little story with you, which I'm sure you'll appreciate. At about 9 am one morning, I was at the gym and one of the trainers – I kid you not – walked through the weights area with a big bag of McDonald's and a can of Red Bull. He sat in a corner and proceeded to eat his breakfast. Now I'm all up for eating whatever you want in moderation, but there is a big difference between competence and excellence.

Another example is learning the Adobe programs to help with your technical design ability, which you can do via online or offline classes, versus an experienced designer or creative director who can do that plus give constructive criticism on your design thinking and idea generation. Maybe even teach you a few things when presenting to clients.

I've also found that, traditionally, mentors don't exchange their time for money, unlike instructors, coaches or consultants. I'll go back to what mentors do get in return later in this book.

> IF YOU COULD ONLY SENSE HOW IMPORTANT YOU ARE TO THE LIVES OF THOSE YOU MEET.
>
> — FRED ROGERS

SO HERE'S HOW YOU FIND ONE:
# THE 12 KEY STEPS TO MENTORSHIP

*Estimated section reading time: 5 minutes / completion time: 30 minutes*

# STEP 1: WRITE A PROMISE LETTER

**The very first thing you need to do is make a conscious decision to commit to and trust in this process.**

The best way I've found to do this is to get a piece of paper and pen, and physically write a personal promise to yourself and at least one person who means the world to you. If you'd like to include me in the written promise, to add weight to the letter (or if you simply don't have anyone reliable), by all means do it.

The words below are an example; in fact, the promise below is my own and you can absolutely take it word for word and use it. Most of my students have and it is perfectly fine. All that matters is that you believe it for yourself and fully understand that you are 100%

accountable. Those you list are counting on you to follow through.

It's essentially a commitment letter to yourself, to solidify your intention on the journey to getting a mentor.

Please take your time with writing this. Don't rush it. Mean every word. You're carving your intentions into a physical artefact. It's the first step to expanding your reality of 'better'.

## YOUR PERSONAL PROMISE LETTER

*<Date in full>*

*I <full name> make a promise to start anew.*

*I promise to leave everything that has kept me back from achieving greatness behind me. To strip away every cell of fear and doubt in my mind and fill it with bravery and inevitable certainty.*

*In order to reach my goals, I have a lot to learn. In order to learn, I am willing to fail. I am willing to work as bad as I want to breathe. I am willing to be uncomfortable in order to succeed. "No" does not exist, only "No, not yet". Because I understand this, I also understand that persistence trumps circumstance.*

*I am completely immersed in this decision and committed to going the distance. I accept that the only magic pill is hard work. Paired with the guidance of this book, I know that the hard work will be amplified in the right direction. <Loved one's name(s) here> and Ram are counting on me. I deeply believe my goals are possible.*

*If not now, then when?*

*Above all, I promise to take action, starting with the steps in Ram's book on getting a mentor.*

*I'm ready. I'm all in.*

*<Sign it with your full name>*

# WHAT'S NEXT?

Once you've written your personal promise letter on a blank piece of paper, you need to take a photo of it and send it to those you included as people who will hold you accountable. If you included me, direct message the photo of it to me privately via Instagram to my handle: @TheGiantThinker so I know you've made the commitment for yourself.

Then, you need to keep that original letter and place it somewhere visible. This is important. So put it next to your computer. Make copies of it and stick it up on the wall. Frame it and put it next to your bed. Stick it on the mirror. Wherever you like. But you need to see it daily so it disrupts your physiological pattern often.

# END OF STEP 1 CHECKLIST

- [ ] I hand wrote my personal promise letter.

- [ ] I internally committed to my promise.

- [ ] I took a photo of my letter.

- [ ] I sent the photo to my accountability network.

- [ ] I photocopied duplicates of my letter and stuck it around my room and desk.

—

# HAVING A MENTOR HAS BUILT MY CONFIDENCE TO REACH FOR WHAT USED TO SEEM IMPOSSIBLE.

— VIVIAN THAM,
PEOPLE AND CULTURE COORDINATOR,
@VIVIAN_TOOKIECLOTHESPIN

—

*Estimated section reading time: 5 minutes / completion time: 20 minutes*

# STEP 2: WHO ARE YOU?

**You need to define your baseline. In this step, you identify your story, also known as your current state. Write down and specify what you're made of. I'll guide you through this with suggested questions.**

I've made room for you to write answers directly. An alternative to this, if you prefer, is writing the question in the middle of a blank page in your notepad and writing answers in a mind map format. Basically, words or short sentence answers around the question.

We'll dig up thoughts around how you grew up and what experiences you can leverage as a unique part of your identity, what you're doing now and why you're doing it. After doing this, you'll be able to better define your purpose in your job role and, more importantly, as a human in this universe. You need to establish your baseline as a brand and as a service.

You and I aren't simply here in this world to exist. So, dig deeper than the superficial by noting your personal values and characteristics that are important to you.

When you know who you are, you can better define what you want. And when you pinpoint what you want, you can then flesh out the necessary steps for how to get there.

The only wrong answer here is if you're not honest. Go wild. Brain dump.

# HERE ARE MY SUGGESTED QUESTIONS DIVIDED INTO TWO AREAS.

**Past:**

- Where are you from? Elk Rapids, MI
- How did you grow up? On a farm — great childhood.
- What country are your parents from originally? USA
- What do/did your parents do for work? Farmers — mom is now part time @ a plant nursery
- How about your grandparents? All are deceased. One doctor, 1 war vet,
- What is your fondest childhood memory? Vacations in the FL Keys
- What were three hobbies or activities you enjoyed when you were a kid in primary/elementary school? Sports (soccer/softball), playing outside, art
- How about high school? Sports (soccer/vball/tennis), art, hanging w/ friends
- What are three achievements you're most proud of?
  ① Being good @ sports (soccer/tennis mainly)
- Have you travelled interstate or overseas? If so, where? Ireland, London, Jamaica, Cancun, Bahamas, FL, Tennesee, Cali, Connecticut, Illinois, Utah, NY

**Present:** → ② Being artistic and known for it
③ Running 2 marathons

- How old are you? 30

- What three hobbies or activities do you enjoy now?
  - Drawing/painting         — acupuncture
  - Working out              — COOKING
  - Various outdoor activities depending on weather
  - Hanging w/ friends

- What city or country are you living in at the moment? Spring Lake, MI — USA

- What are you learning at the moment? How to improve myself — holistic health
- Where do you work and what do you do there? Designvox — graphic designer
- If you're a student, where and what are you studying? N/A

- What are you creating right now or have created recently? Various art projects (invites/logos) Work: brochures/websites/print pieces
- What habitual activities are part of your daily routine? cooking/food prep, working out, fertility crap
- What do you feel are two or three of your character-based strengths? Generally optimistic, empathetic, creative
- What are your two or three character-based weaknesses? Lack confidence, easily distracted
- What are you most passionate about? Being healthy — improving my life + the ppl. around me
- What's one thing that you can't go a day without thinking about? Babies

- What gets you excited? Being inspired, hanging w/ friends, potential pregnancy
- What are three personal values or traits that a loved one or family member might note about you? I'm empathetic, good listener, kind, fun
- If you had the attention of the entire human race for 10 seconds, what would you say?

Be kind to yourself and those around you. Always seek to inspire and be inspired.

This is a personal analysis to pinpoint exactly where you are. You need to do this in order to map out the blueprint of everything you'd like to achieve moving forward.

With this step, all the way to step 6, make sure that you're not writing full paragraphs. Use dot points. Keep the answers short. If they are sentences, that's fine, but be succinct and get straight to the point. No waffling. Be brutally honest with yourself in your answers.

Be specific. The more specific your answers are, the easier it'll be to get the right mentors tailored to your needs.

# END OF STEP 2 CHECKLIST

- [✓] I wrote dot points about who I was in the past.
- [✓] I wrote dot points about who I am currently.
- [✓] I have a clear understanding of my personal values, characteristics and what's important to me.

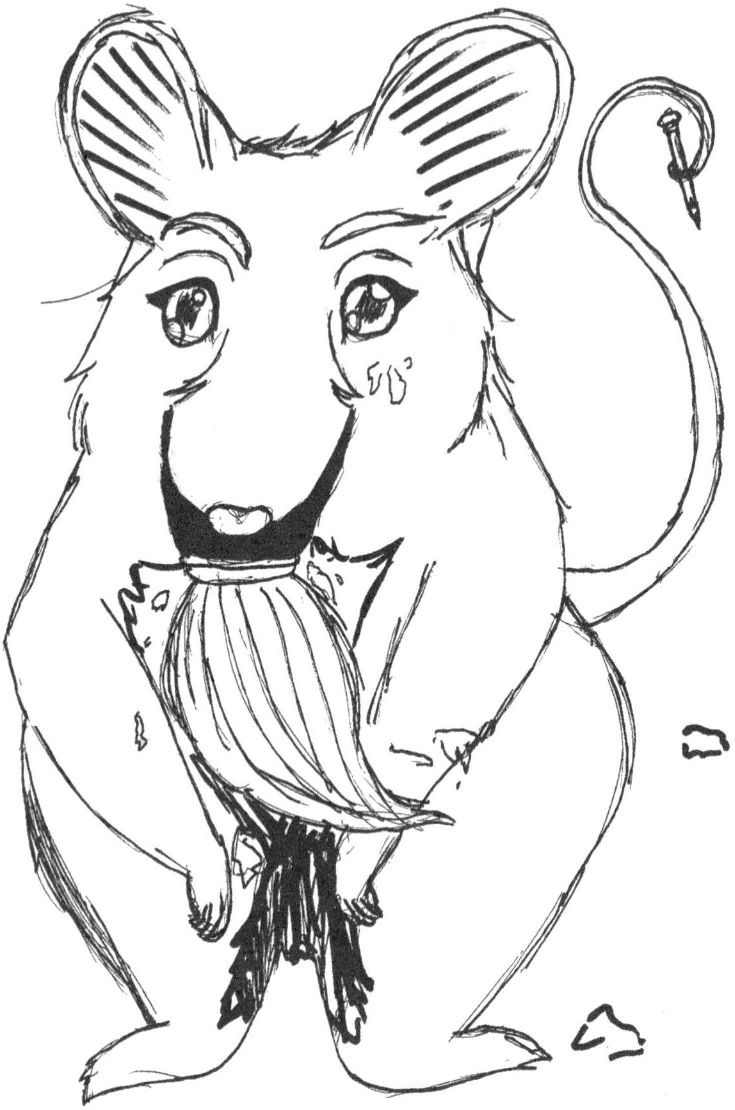

# GETTING A MENTOR WOULD BREAK DOWN BARRIERS AND INSPIRE ME TO TAKE CHANCES.

— BECKA LUKENS,
GRAPHIC DESIGNER & PHOTOGRAPHER

*Estimated short story reading time: 5 minutes*

# WHAT I LEARNT FROM A FORMER DESIGN DIRECTOR OF HASBRO

At the beginning of 2015 I returned from my first three-month USA speaking tour. I visited 22 cities, experienced the diversity of America and engaged with over 10,000+ people, in an attempt to share the lessons documented in my first book *How to get a job as a designer, guaranteed.*

One of the many highlights during that trip was having a private lunch with Gary Smith, Vice-President of Product Design and Development at Herman Miller, after delivering a keynote speech to the company. As you may know, Herman Miller created the famous Aeron chair, Marshmallow sofa and the Eames lounge chair.

Gary Smith was also previously the Design Director for Hasbro in the 80s and was hugely responsible for the creation of Mr Potato Head, G.I. Joe and My Little Pony. He could even freely sketch the outline of the first My Little Pony design on a napkin with a pen.

During our lunch conversation, one story I'd like to share is about Gary and his seven-year-old son. One afternoon, Gary was teaching his son how to paint. The subject matter was a deer.

As they both started painting away, Gary's son began to get frustrated that his painting was just blobs of paint and it didn't look like a deer like his father's. Gary then asked his son, "What is a deer?" His son just looked at him, perplexed and confused.

Then Gary went on to say, "Don't paint the deer, paint what the deer is."

Now before his son could bail, Gary picked up his brush, dabbed a bit of paint and continued with, "What is a deer? A deer is powerful, graceful and majestic – so paint this. A deer isn't violent, erratic or hot tempered – so don't paint the deer that way ... paint what the deer is."

**So the question I ask you is, "What are you?"**

What are you, really?

Because what you hold in your hands is more valuable than what money could ever buy, and I'm not referring to the piece of paper you collected (or will soon collect) as your name echoed in that graduation ceremony once upon a time.

I'm referring to your abilities. Trust in them. Although seemingly premature, they are bursting to solve problems, to flood the world with simplicity, with beauty, with entertainment, with innovation and most of all, with value.

You have a gift.

You have a responsibility.

You are one of the thinkers, the doers and the makers of right now.

You are light in a world that can sometimes seem dark.

You matter.

And the world needs you.

**When you believe that you truly have value in the world, you realise that you have an obligation to deliver it. Give yourself permission to do this.**

Try not to fall into the trap of settling for safe or living a life based on the expectations of others. Look inward. You've already tasted what you really enjoy doing.

What you want is sacred. It's fragile and can be taken from you in a whisper. Protect it. Stay in that sanctuary. The vibration within you is real.

*Estimated section reading time: 10 minutes / completion time: 60 minutes*

# STEP 3: WHAT DO YOU WANT?

**In this step, you write down and define your goals. They must be outcome-based, specific and measurable. I've suggested questions to guide you below. You can write your answers directly after them.**

There's power in vision and imagination. It's what makes us different to any other living being on the planet. The ability to imagine and project into the future a reality that hasn't actually happened yet, even when there's no physical evidence to suggest that it's possible, is a switch that we can all flick on anytime.

An obvious example that comes to mind is the first flight by the Wright brothers:

*Reference: http://www.eyewitnesstohistory.com/wright.htm*

*"On December 17, 1903, Orville Wright piloted the first powered airplane 20 feet above a wind-swept beach in North Carolina. The flight lasted 12 seconds and covered 120 feet. Three more flights were made that day with Orville's brother Wilbur piloting the record flight lasting 59 seconds over a distance of 852 feet."*

So what are you working towards? What are your short-, mid- and long-term visions?

I suggest you choose one primary goal for each category suggested below, divided into short-, mid- and long-term timeframes. Focusing on these nine core goals, scattered over a digestible period of time, will minimise the potential of feeling overwhelmed. Having too many goals can also distract you and you'll end up achieving none of them.

But a goal of simply 'getting a mentor' is not specific enough. You have to define what type of mentor. What does that ideal mentor look like? Who is it? Where are they? What do they stand for? What are his or her peers like? These thoughts will set in stone what you want, and indirectly, what you don't want.

Simply 'being happy' is definitely not measurable. What experiences would tick that box for you?

Perhaps it's travelling to a specific country, winning a particular industry-related award or helping a community in need. Write down the people, places and things that would make you happy.

How about finances? Don't say you want to be rich; instead write down an exact dollar amount you'd like to earn as a salary, or an amount you'd like to save. And of course, when you write that you want a job or more clients or 'to take my career or business to the next level', you must specify exactly what that next level looks like.

'Getting a job' is certainly not specific enough. You must define what job. Where is it and what is the culture of that organisation?

Defining what you want includes both internal goals and external goals.

You see, it's impossible for a soccer player to kick a goal without goal posts. He or she would then be kicking a ball to nowhere. This is the exact same thing. Put those goal posts up by defining exactly what you want. Visualise your target in high definition, rather than blurred pixels.

Most of the problems I had in the past with not getting what I wanted stemmed from lack of clarity.

Here are my suggested questions divided into three categories.

## PERSONAL GOALS:

- What weaknesses would you like to turn into strengths?
- What are your characteristic attribute goals?
- What are your value goals?
- What are your relationship goals?

## PROFESSIONAL GOALS:

- What are your conceptual skill goals?
- What are your technical skill goals?
- What are your financial goals?
- What are your career or business goals?

# PHYSICAL GOALS:

- What are your health and fitness goals?
- What are your lifestyle goals?
- What are your object goals?

**After you've warmed up with the above lists of goals, you need to curate and prioritise them into timeframes within those categories.** Let's start with short-term goals, which are goals with a three-month timeframe. Choose one primary goal from each category: personal, professional and physical:

My three-month primary *personal* goal is …

_____

_____

My three-month primary *professional* goal is …

_____

_____

My three-month primary *physical* goal is …

_____

_____

## THREE-MONTH TIMEFRAME = SHORT-TERM

| Primary goals guide |||
|---|---|---|
| 1 x personal | 1 x professional | 1 x physical |

| Secondary goals guide |||
|---|---|---|
| 1 x personal | 1 x professional | 1 x physical |

## ONE-YEAR TIMEFRAME = MID-TERM

| Primary goals guide |||
|---|---|---|
| 1 x personal | 1 x professional | 1 x physical |

| Secondary goals guide |||
|---|---|---|
| 1 x personal | 1 x professional | 1 x physical |

## THREE-YEAR TIMEFRAME = LONG-TERM

| Primary goals guide |||
|---|---|---|
| 1 x personal | 1 x professional | 1 x physical |

| Secondary goals guide |||
|---|---|---|
| 1 x personal | 1 x professional | 1 x physical |

**YOU NEED TO 'START WITH THE END IN MIND'. WHEN YOU DO THAT, YOU CAN REVERSE ENGINEER THE NECESSARY STEPS TO GET THERE.**

— RAM CASTILLO

# END OF STEP 3 CHECKLIST

☐ I brainstormed a list of personal goals I want to achieve.

☐ I brainstormed a list of professional goals I want to achieve.

☐ I brainstormed a list of physical goals I want to achieve.

☐ I curated and populated my primary goals in the relevant categories and timeframes, using or referencing the table provided.

**HEY, GOOD JOB!
YOU'VE COMPLETED 25%
LET'S KEEP AT IT.**

**3 OUT OF 12 STEPS COMPLETE**

*Estimated section reading time: 5 minutes / completion time: 30 minutes*

# STEP 4: WHY DO YOU WANT IT?

**In this step, you match each goal with powerful reasons as to why you want it. I'll guide you.**

Start thinking about what you feel each goal you have listed will enable.

Here's another lens to look through: What will it cost you if you don't follow through? How will it affect you and the people around you if you continue on the same route you're on right now? What will happen to your emotional, mental, physical, financial, spiritual and creative health if you don't meet these listed goals?

Remember, not making a decision is a decision. So in your written answers, include the consequences of what will happen if you remain in your current state.

I recommend that you put a lot on the line here. If you say you want to be a designer or reach a level of seniority, but you're not sure why, then you won't last long or progress further in the industry. In fact, you'll likely not even finish your course if you're just starting out. Or you may easily throw in the towel when you're under pressure once you're at that higher level.

On the other hand, if you understand the power design has on influencing human behaviour and you use that power to help make people's lives better, easier, more valuable and more enjoyable, it will give you the nourishment and sustenance to overcome any obstacle.

The main reason why people don't follow through or just give up is because they have either skipped this step or haven't gone deep enough.

**Complete these sentences for all short-, mid- and long-term primary goals. Let's start with the 'why' answer for the three-month timeframe:**

My three-month primary *personal* goal is …
I want this because …

_____

_____

_____


My three-month primary *professional* goal is …
I want this because …

_____

_____

_____


My three-month primary *physical* goal is …
I want this because …

_____

_____

_____

# END OF STEP 4 CHECKLIST

☐ I wrote why I wanted my primary goal for each category, starting with the short-term timeframe.

☐ I wrote why I wanted my primary goal for each category within the mid-term timeframe.

☐ I wrote why I wanted my primary goal for each category within the long-term timeframe.

☐ Each of my nine primary goals is now matched with a powerful reason as to why I want it.

**TAKE THREE**
# DEEP BREATHS

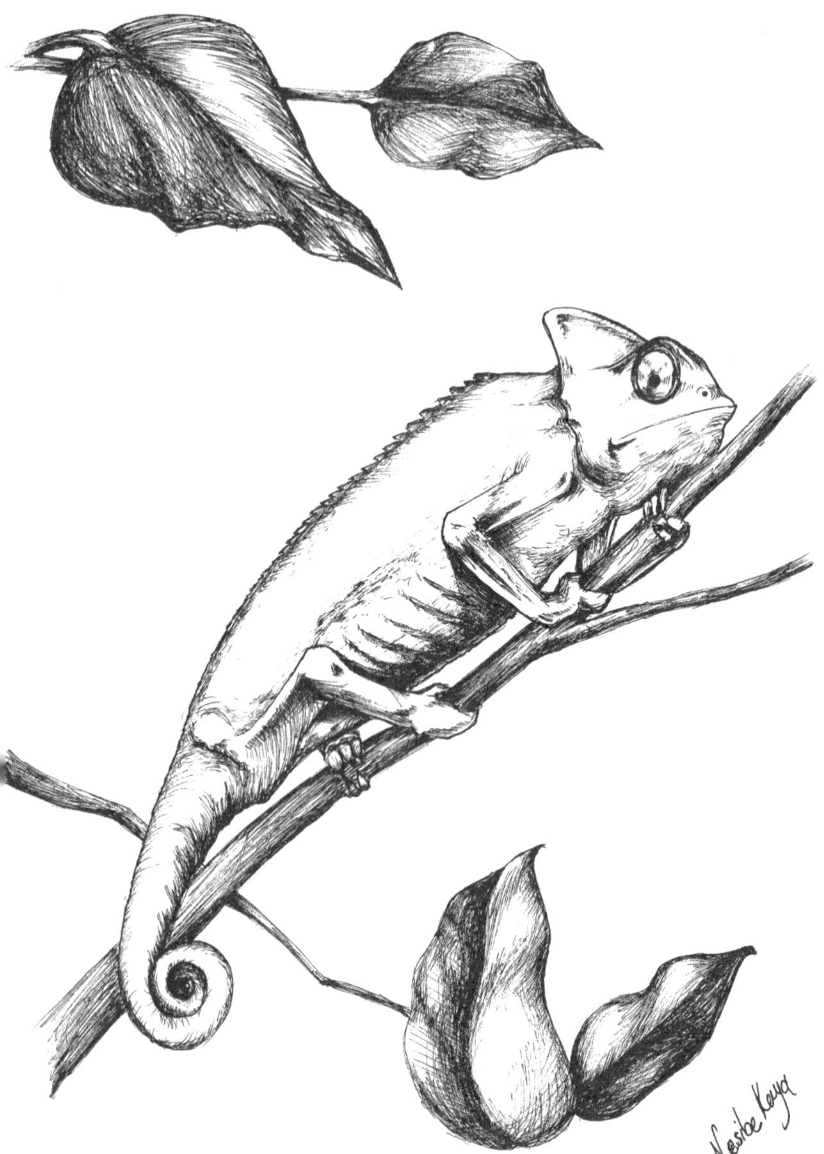

—

# GETTING A MENTOR WOULD HELP ME TO HARMONISE WITH NEW CONDITIONS.

— NESIBE KAYA, INDUSTRIAL DESIGN STUDENT, @SKETCHESOFCHINDIMPLE

—

*Estimated section reading time: 5 minutes / completion time: 30 minutes*

# STEP 5: WHAT'S STOPPING YOU FROM GETTING IT?

**This step involves writing down all the things that you feel are holding you back. Every single one of them. I'll help you navigate through this.**

We need to match each primary goal listed in step 3 with the specific perceived obstacles that are stopping you from reaching that goal.

**Common obstacles:**

- being time-poor
- lack of money
- fear (of failure, rejection, disappointment etc.)
- lack of self-confidence
- lack of knowledge
- not having enough connections.

**Complete these sentences for all short-, mid- and long-term primary goals. Let's start with the 'obstacles' answers for the three-month timeframe:**

Regarding my three-month primary ***personal*** goal, the following is what I feel is stopping me from getting it …

_____

_____

Regarding my three-month primary ***professional*** goal, the following is what I feel is stopping me from getting it …

_____

_____

Regarding my three-month primary ***physical*** goal, the following is what I feel is stopping me from getting it …

_____

_____

**Once you've answered the above, we'll then pair them up with actionable solutions in step 6.**

# END OF STEP 5 CHECKLIST

☐ I wrote what's stopping me from achieving my primary goal for each category starting with the short-term timeframe.

☐ I wrote what's stopping me from achieving my primary goal for each category within the mid-term timeframe.

☐ I wrote what's stopping me from achieving my primary goal for each category within the long-term timeframe.

☐ Each of my nine primary goals is now matched with a reason for what I feel is stopping me from getting it.

> **MENTORS ARE HUMAN TOO. SOMETIMES WE CAN FORGET THAT.**
>
> — RAM CASTILLO

**5 OUT OF 12 STEPS COMPLETE**

*Estimated section reading time: 5 minutes  /  completion time: 30 minutes*

# STEP 6: HOW CAN YOU OVERCOME IT?

**In this step, you pair each obstacle item you wrote in step 5 with a solution.**

Here's another way of re-framing it:

If you could overcome each specific barrier, what would it look like?

If you could overcome each specific barrier, what actions must be taken to bridge the gap?

If you're sceptical about this, humour yourself for just a moment and try it anyway. What would it take to overcome each barrier?

Remember the common obstacles listed in the previous step? Below are some example solutions to them.

## BEING TIME-POOR

Everyone has 24 hours in a day; prioritise yours. Stop watching Netflix or *The Bachelor*. Stop playing games. Stop talking about 'how you're going to do it' when you hang out with friends at a pub or cafe. And stop scrolling through Facebook every 10 minutes. If you're under 25 and still live with your parents, you, my friend, are in the best position. Time is not a renewable resource and you would have the most of it. If you're over 25, chin up. We've got more of something else. It's called life experience.

Did you know… *"Even during low frequency hours 3-5 a.m. ET, when 24 percent of Lockets users are actively swiping, the average user checks his or her phone four times an hour. BuzzFeed noted that 110 checks a day spread over 12 hours is one glimpse every six or seven minutes."*

*Reference: http://www.idigitaltimes.com/how-often-do-you-check-your-phone-locket-app-data-shows-users-unlock-smartphone-110-times-day-364787*

## LACK OF MONEY

Work, save and use what's freely available. Listen, you have to be resourceful. You can either work a few extra casual shifts, do some odd jobs for others or find free ways to achieve your goals. For example if you can't go to design college, there are plenty of free online resources to start learning. Free information can be a solution to many obstacles. I've included a resources list at the end of the book.

## FEAR (OF FAILURE, REJECTION, DISAPPOINTMENT)

Failure is necessary for growth. What is the worst that can happen? Living with regret is far more painful.

## LACK OF SELF-CONFIDENCE

Do you want to be more confident in your interviews? Or even general interactions? Besides tips online, you may want to role-play with someone with experience or a business owner friend of your parents, to practise face-to-face situations.

## LACK OF KNOWLEDGE

Research, find some mentors, volunteer yourself, participate online and offline and up-skill only to the minimum required amount of that goal.

## NOT ENOUGH CONNECTIONS

One common obstacle is not knowing the right people. Notice I say 'right people'. The right people in my experience have been two types of groups. One group show you the door, the other group help you on the other side after you've walked through it. Lack of connections is often a result of undefined targets. Plant seeds and knock on doors online.

**There's always a way to getting the mentor, the job, the client, the project and the experience you want. It simply comes down to unwavering, consistent action, and how badly you want it. You only lose when you give up. So don't.**

**Complete these sentences for all short-, mid- and long-term primary goals:**

With what's stopping me from achieving my three-month primary *personal* goal, I can overcome it by ...

_____

_____

_____


With what's stopping me from achieving my three-month primary *professional* goal, I can overcome it by ...

_____

_____

_____


With what's stopping me from achieving my three-month primary *physical* goal, I can overcome it by ...

_____

_____

_____

# END OF STEP 6 CHECKLIST

☐ Starting with the short-term timeframe, I wrote solutions to each obstacle stopping me from achieving my primary goal within each category.

☐ I wrote solutions to each obstacle stopping me from achieving my primary goal within the mid-term timeframe.

☐ I wrote solutions to each obstacle stopping me from achieving my primary goal within the long-term timeframe.

☐ Each of my nine primary goals is now matched with solutions to obstacles that I felt were stopping me.

# 50%

**WOOT! HALF-WAY MARK!
YOU'VE COMPLETED 50%
LET'S KEEP THE MOMENTUM.**

*Estimated section reading time: 5 minutes / completion time: 30 minutes*

# STEP 7: GATHER THE BEST PEOPLE

**This is a listing exercise. Write down everyone who comes to mind who embodies all of (or at least some of) the qualities of your targeted goals. I'll guide your grouping of these people in this step.**

Make sure to list real people, not movie characters – don't put Tyler Durden from *Fight Club*, Jack Sparrow from *Pirates of the Caribbean* or Elsa from *Frozen* on there. And you don't need to know these people personally.

I repeat … you don't need to know these people personally. Big one! This leads to my strong recommendation to gather a list of people well beyond your local proximity.

Who we spend time with is who we'll become. And who do we spend most of our time with? Those we love: our friends and family. And how did they come to us? We went to school with them, we worked with them at some point, we enjoyed their company socially. That's all well and good but they shouldn't necessarily be our teachers. The mistake most people make is that they only learn from people within their proximity.

For example, I wanted the ability to free up more time and create systems like Tim Ferriss. I wanted to hustle like Gary Vaynerchuk. I wanted to put people over profit like Dale Partridge. I wanted to be able to connect with people on stage like Anthony Robbins. I wanted to create a podcast that was honest and helpful like Pat Flynn. And I wanted to work extremely hard, just like my father.

Who the mentor is will be a direct result of the goals you've set, because they must have already achieved it themselves. The goal you've set will be a direct result of your personal values. You can see why this entire process is so important. It may seem long, but in my experience, each step is necessary. This trail (consciously or even unconsciously) is an attempt to align with your version of success, contribution and ultimately happiness.

**Group the names under one of the three connection status categories:**

1. I have zero connection to them.

2. I am connected to them through a mutual friend.

3. I have a direct connection to them.

Mentors are everywhere. It's important to have more than one. This list of prospective mentors you admire even have mentors themselves.

# END OF STEP 7 CHECKLIST

☐ I wrote down everyone who comes to mind who embodies the qualities in my targeted goals.

☐ I distributed each person to one of the three connection status category options presented.

☐ I'm convinced that, to my knowledge, I have gathered the best people as prospective mentors, even if I have zero connection to them right now.

STAND TALL AND
**STRETCH**

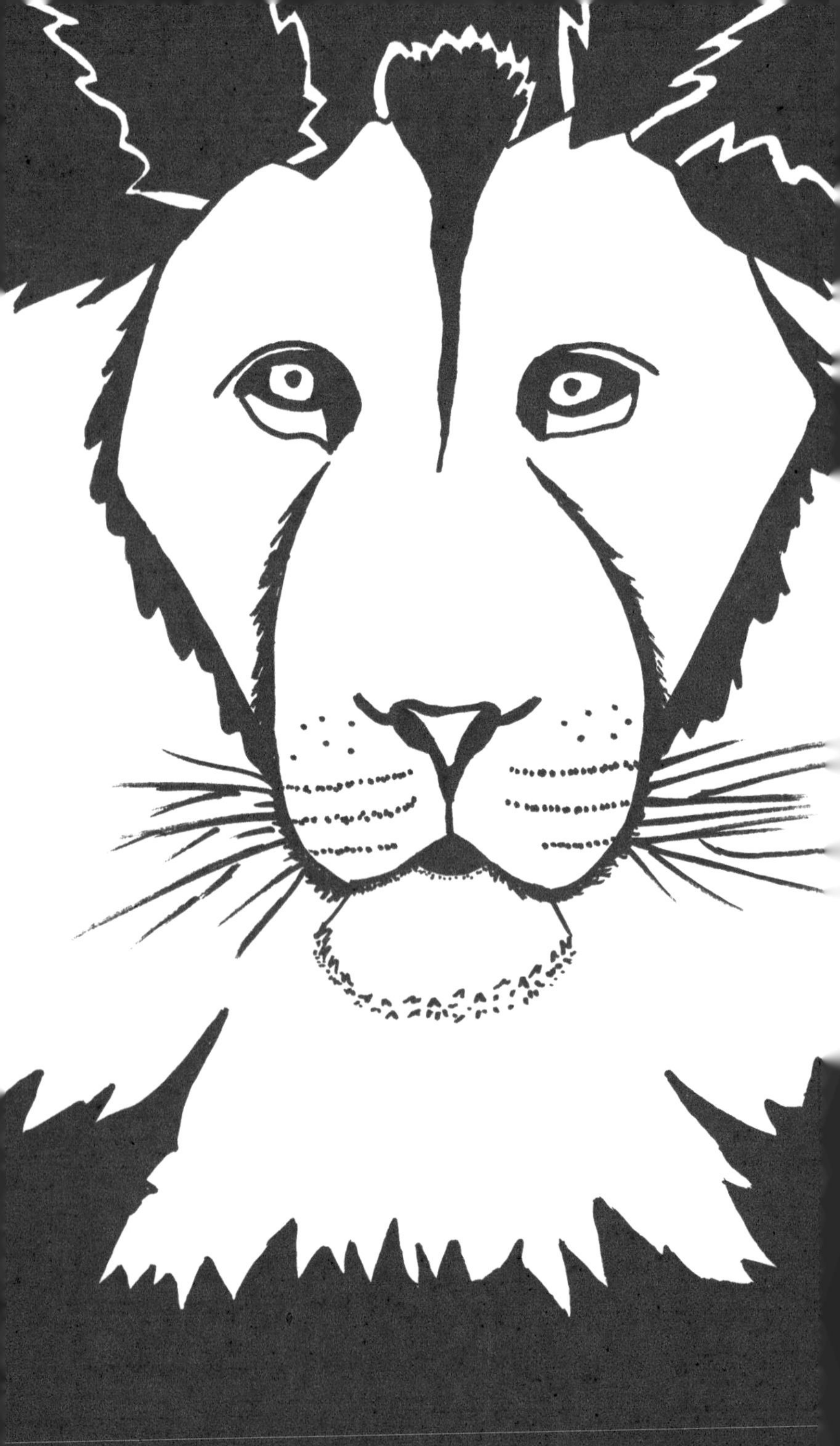

## GETTING A MENTOR WOULD EMPOWER ME.

— ASHLEY SPERRY, GRAPHIC DESIGNER, WRITER AND ILLUSTRATOR, @ASHLEYSPERRYBIZ

*Estimated section reading time: 5 minutes / completion time: 30 minutes*

# STEP 8: PAIR EACH PERSON YOU'VE GATHERED TO EACH APPROPRIATE GOAL

**In this step, you have to assess which of your primary goals would be fast-tracked with the help of the people you listed in step 7.**

More than one person should be listed under each goal. And, you can allocate the same person to more than one goal if it's relevant.

Don't limit yourself by thinking "this isn't realistic" or "this person won't want to mentor me". This is a pairing exercise, so stay focused on that.

You need to push beyond your reality because your reality is often an accumulation of what you've achieved and experienced to date. Human nature is geared toward survival instincts. The unknown raises red flags of fear due to uncertainty. Fear can cripple or it can empower. If you really want an unbiased view of it, see fear for what it is, not worse than it is.

I'd like to describe fear as false constructs, built on untested assumptions. Fear is often pointing you to where you need to go, not the other way around. It's uncomfortable. I know. But this is good. It's when the most growth happens. Seth Godin once said that "the lessons we remember are the lessons we learn the hard way" and Anthony Robbins complements this with his quote "we're meant to grow so we have something to give".

Newness and shooting for the seemingly impossible really does sound crazy at first! I hear you. But as Henry Ford once said, "If I asked people what they wanted, they would say faster horses". We wouldn't have cars if it weren't for people like Henry. You've no doubt heard or read that quote many times before, and there's a reason why it retains impact.

**Complete these sentences for all short-, mid- and long-term primary goals. Let's start with the 'pairings' for the three-month timeframe:**

Assisting my three-month primary *personal* goal, the following people could be great mentors…

_____

_____

_____

Assisting my three-month primary *professional* goal, the following people could be great mentors…

_____

_____

_____

Assisting my three-month primary *physical* goal, the following people could be great mentors…

_____

_____

_____

# END OF STEP 8 CHECKLIST

☐ I revisited my nine primary goals.

☐ I allocated my gathered list of prospective mentors to one or more primary goal, starting with my primary goals for the short-term timeframe.

☐ I paired my prospective mentors to one or more primary goal within the mid-term timeframe.

☐ I paired my prospective mentors to one or more primary goal within the long-term timeframe.

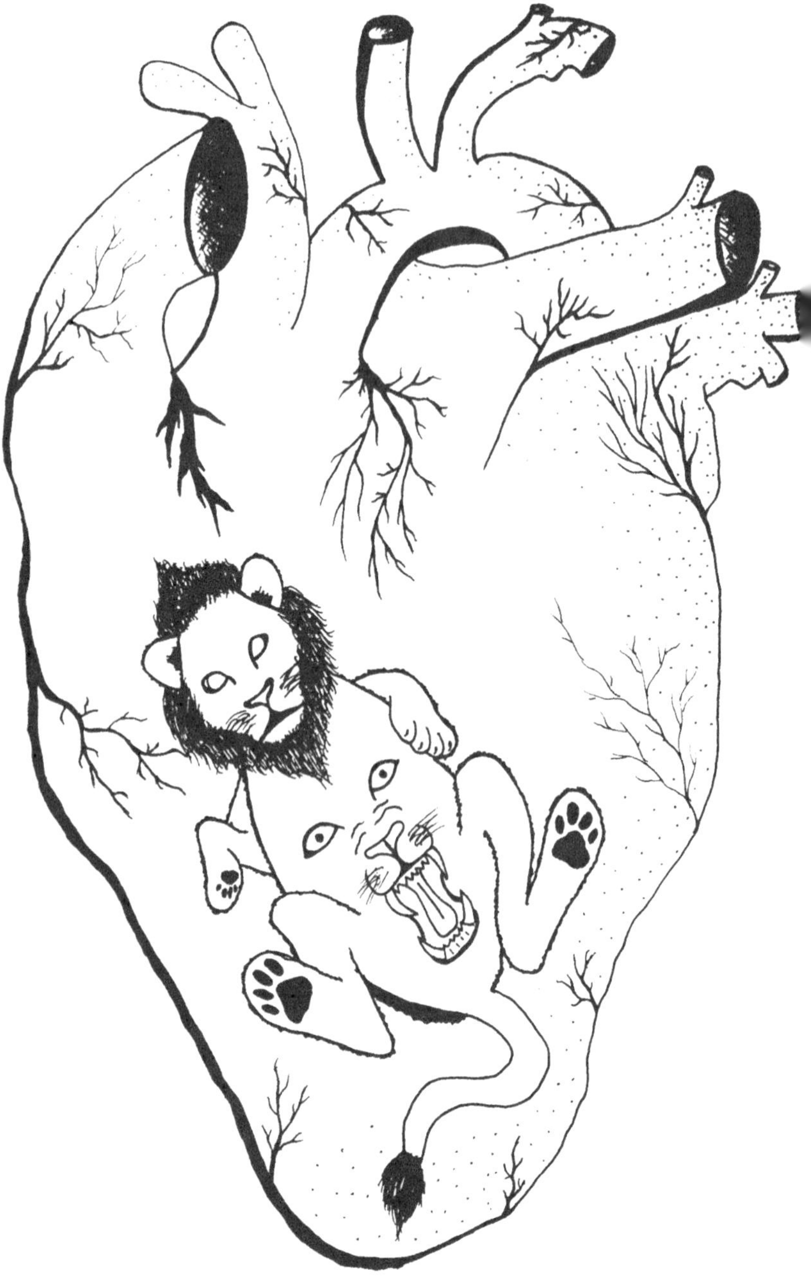

# GETTING A MENTOR WOULD AWAKEN THE LION INSIDE MY HEART.

— JOSÉ HERNÁNDEZ TRUJILLO,
GRAPHIC DESIGNER,
@GRAFISTAJH

*Estimated section reading time: 30 minutes / completion time: 90 minutes*

# STEP 9: IDENTIFY THE STRATEGY TO REACH THEM, FOLLOWED BY THE PLAN TO ENABLE IT

**Strategy means 'what are you going to do?' The idea is that you're currently at A, you've defined B and C, and acknowledge you need to get to those destinations. Essentially, outline the desired outcomes in sequence.**

To start, get one pairing you did in step 8 (one primary goal and one person you've matched it with). Now, let's reverse engineer the criteria required for him or her to help you achieve that goal.

**Plan means 'how are you going to do it?' How will you move from A to B to C? What are the best vehicles to take you there?**

I know this may seem confusing if this is the first time you've done this. Rest assured, I'll help you through it. You're doing great! You've made it to step 9!

Below are simple examples of this 'strategy meets plan' relationship. Feel free to include it in yours or build upon it.

### 1. Demonstrate adequate design credibility:

- Build an online design portfolio (or update it) showing your best work to date.
- Complete your LinkedIn profile.
- Upskill if necessary.
- Include a list of completed courses or design related awards on all online profile bios and your resume.

## 2. Show enthusiasm towards design and your professional development:

- Identify professional development related goals and make them public. This includes your career objective on your bio and CV. Plus, if the opportunity arises, in online and offline conversation.

- Broadcast your design related interest on Facebook, Instagram, Twitter and Snapchat. This could include what you recently learnt or achieved. It could be challenges you're facing which your network could engage with and have a point of view on. Or simply a current update of your professional development progress after a class, course, book, workshop or conference you've completed.

- Ask questions within an area of design interest online and offline (this includes using the comments feature at the end of blog posts, reddit threads, forums, anchor.fm and Q&A segments during live events).

- Create content consistently on design topics of interest. This could include writing an article hosted on your blog or medium.com, a short vlog-style video posted on YouTube or Facebook, or commentary and reflections which you can post on other social media channels.

- Actively engage in design related events and talk about them to people you interact with afterwards.

### 3. Build substantial rapport:

- If appropriate, ask for one method of contact information upon meeting someone. LinkedIn or email always works with little to no hesitation. Needless to say, we can't build rapport with someone without an introduction and a contact exchange.
- Follow up with gratitude and appreciation using the contact channel available to you.
- Find commonalities, leverage them and include them in conversation.
- Acknowledge opinions and actively listen in each interaction (rather than talking all the time).

Above are indicative examples only. Each strategy item and action will differ depending on the goal-to-prospective-mentor pairing. Repeat this step for each pairing.

# GIVE FIRST, RATHER THAN TAKE. MAKE FRIENDS, NOT CONTACTS. HELP OTHERS BEFORE YOURSELF.

You might actually find that the strategy for one pairing could be as simple as point 3 mentioned previously: 'build substantial rapport'. You could be in a position where you've already met that person once or twice but have never engaged them in a mentor to mentee context. Maybe you've been introduced by a mutual friend who has already spoken highly of you, conveniently ticking the 'credibility' and 'enthusiasm' boxes for you. The required action on your end could then be to send them an email or private message on social media, starting with a simple hello. Re-engage and go from there. Don't overthink the strategy and plan. Keep it simple.

Conversely, they may be quite well-known in the public eye and difficult to reach. The rapport component would need a lot more investment of your time and participation, likely a long endeavour to ensure that the person gradually gets to know you. This could look like a year or more of heavy social media engagement between you and all their content.

**Including:**

- re-tweeting
- replying to their tweets

- 'snapping' comments or observations directly to their Snapchat or commenting on their Instagram stories
- commenting on their Instagram posts or direct messaging them
- sharing their Facebook content
- participating on their Facebook live sessions or Periscopes
- thanking them and informing them via email that you tried their advice on their latest blog post.

Imagine if someone did this to you? Not nagging them with endless questions, but rather truly engaging with them in dialogue. You can see why this will pay off. You become top of mind to this person. You show the enthusiasm, as mentioned earlier. Beyond that, you show all the qualities mentors feed off and need to refuel with themselves.

# THREE POWER TIPS:

**1. Find communication platforms your prospective mentors use, that aren't overly crowded:**

How did I chat one-on-one with TV's *Shark Tank* US investor and NBA Dallas Maverick's owner Mark Cuban? I used a platform that he created that wasn't widely used at the time. It's a messaging app called Cyber Dust.

**2. Find what you can do to help them:**

Some examples include volunteering to help organise an event they will be speaking at or interviewing them for your podcast or blog, which would expose them to a new audience.

**3. Participate when they go live:**

Whether it's on Facebook live, Periscope or anything that emerges in future, which will enable real-time interaction, joining the conversation often enough will add to significant rapport building.

**Guided by the structure of the previous examples, list the strategy and plan for all short-, mid- and long-term primary goals. Let's start with the goal-to-mentor 'pairings' for the three-month timeframe:**

The strategy and plan to reach my listed prospective mentor, for my three-month primary ***personal*** goal will be the following ...

The strategy and plan to reach my listed prospective mentor, for my three-month primary ***professional*** goal will be the following ...

The strategy and plan to reach my listed prospective mentor, for my three-month primary ***physical*** goal will be the following ...

**This will require more space to write, so feel free to use your notepad, a blank piece of paper or a text file to document your answers.**

# END OF STEP 9 CHECKLIST

- [ ] I fully understand the need to reverse engineer the criteria to reach my prospective mentor.

- [ ] I've outlined what outcomes I need to achieve in sequence to establish an authentic connection and retain a professional relationship with my prospective mentors.

- [ ] Underneath each outcome, I've identified the actions required to bring them to life.

- [ ] I've executed each of those identified actions.

- [ ] I've repeated this entire step for each goal-to-prospective-mentor-pairing.

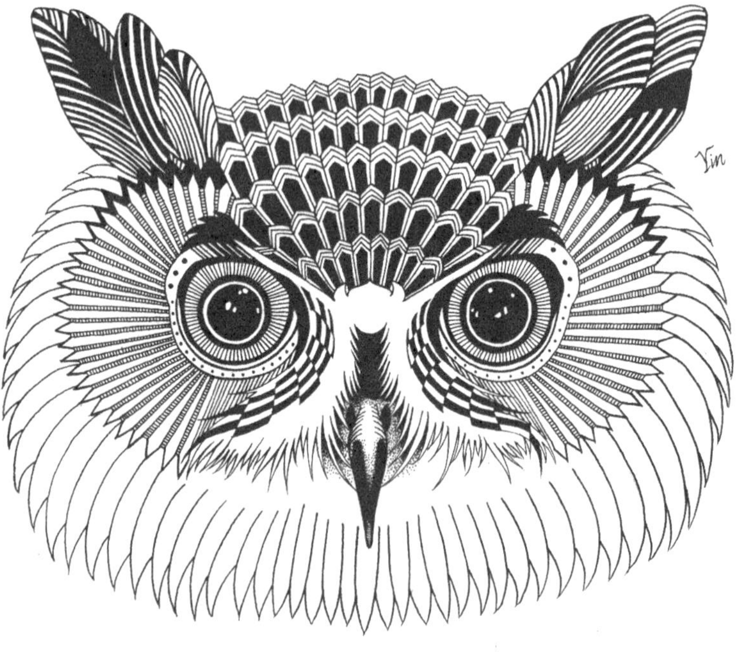
Yin

—

# HAVING A MENTOR WOULD BRING ME WISDOM.

— YIN DUAN,
GRAPHIC DESIGNER AND ILLUSTRATOR,
@HELLOYINDUAN

—

# THE SIX TRAITS THAT WILL MAKE YOU STAND OUT

To empower you in this current step and the remaining three steps to come, you need to recognise that you are already valuable and have value to give. Okay?

This is really important. Because prospective mentors will only mentor you if you give them value in return.

You could be thinking "Yeah, I know that they need value, but what could I possibly offer an expert?"

Notice I said "Recognise that you are already valuable"? What do I mean by this?

The fact that you're reading this book is a perfect example. It shows the following qualities are within you (you just need to believe in it yourself):

- an attitude of gratitude
- a hunger for continuous learning
- a willingness to take initiative
- passionate, with a plan

- enthusiastic to improve
- optimistic towards endless possibilities.

All of this is part of your attitude. And attitude is more valuable than skill. Don't get me wrong, no amount of attitude alone will successfully prepare a medically untrained person to perform brain surgery. Only a skilled and experienced surgeon will be able to do that.

What I'm saying is that attitude comes first. Attitude breeds the longevity required for that surgeon to learn the skills to reach mastery.

Skill is something you can teach and be competent in quite quickly through repetition. Attitude, on the other hand, stems from values, belief systems and personal rules. It's not so easily taught and is really about a person's concrete way of thinking or feeling, typically reflected in their behaviour.

You may already know the importance of this, but is it part of your character? Most of the time it's a simple case of having an open mind, taking a step back and seeing the bigger picture. A small shift in perspective like this will not only draw mentors to you, but you will begin to love challenges and have more energy in your approaches. Below are a few of those characteristics explained in more detail. They will empower you to be more engaging.

## 1. An attitude of gratitude

If you've ever been to a third world country, you'll know what I mean. My mother once told me that "Your absolute worst nightmare is someone else's greatest dream". No matter how bad you've got it, a whole lot of people out there have it much, much worse. Having an attitude of gratitude has helped me re-focus and re-frame many situations in my career, and my life.

In 2008, I went to the Philippines on a holiday and paid an equivalent of $5 AUD for a one-hour back massage. It was the first thing I did when I arrived in my five-star hotel in Makati. The therapist gave me my change and so I tipped about $2 AUD. She then gave it back to me, thinking I didn't know it was my change. I clarified with her that it was for her because she did a great job. She began to cry and said "thank you" repeatedly. She couldn't believe it. And neither could I.

There are many ways to feel grateful; it's all around us.

You wake up and look in the mirror and are alive, for one. The majority of us have arms, legs, ears, eyes, fingers, toes, a heart, a brain and all the necessary functions to perform extraordinary things for ourselves and others.

So when you do feel a little burdened ... on top of life's obstacles you might not be getting those call-backs or finding it difficult to deal with people's responses. Take a moment to pause and think of the abundance of wealth you already have. I bet you could name ten great things in under 30 seconds.

## 2. A hunger for continuous learning

There's nothing more appealing for a mentor than someone who is willing to learn. Too often I find people being technically competent yet aren't sociable. Or worse, over confident and cocky causing huge communication barriers.

Having a hunger for continuous learning works in two ways. You become more valuable and in turn are delivering higher standards of work. You'll also be more approachable and will add to the dynamic culture and morale of the institution and circles you're in.

If you're starting your first design job, you will find yourself crossing over to receptionist or personal assistant roles. This might even be how you get your foot in the door to your design job. This is all part of your learning.

If you need to get coffees, do it. If you need to change light bulbs, do it. If you need to order and stock paper, do it. If you need to start in the mailroom, do it.

I did all these things, and made 350 friends in the office of one of the world's largest advertising networks (Ogilvy). Boy did that pay off in the long term.

**3. A willingness to take initiative**

If you don't know what to do or find yourself stuck (which will be often when you're starting off in any workplace), then find a way. Ask the question to someone who can give you the right answer, Google your queries, post on forums, read relevant books, watch tutorials on YouTube and search on Twitter. There is an abundance of free information out there: all you have to do is look.

Asking quality questions will always give you quality answers.

## 4. Be passionate, with a plan

It's easy to be passionate about design if you have a deep emotional connection with it. Be passionate but informed. It's not enough to just be passionate. Anthony Robbins once said "you can't travel east looking for a sunset, no matter how hard you try, it's never going to happen so have a strategy".

This is where following through comes into play. If you say you're "interested" then show interest, if you say you want to know "how" then find out, if you say you'll "get in touch" then send that email or dial that number. It's that simple. Align your actions with your words.

## 5. Be enthusiastic to improve

You need to show prospective mentors that you're trying. Or as my fellow Aussies say "Have a crack!" Be transparent with your current results and your attempts in going at it alone. This shows that you're not lazy; instead, you've reached a point where you could use their help. Share with your prospective mentors your experiences; what has and hasn't worked.

How active are you as an emerging designer or up-and-comer in your design area of interest? What's your participation level like? Basically what is your online and offline identity saying about you? When someone stumbles on your LinkedIn profile, what will they read? Or how about your Instagram account? What will the experience be like when they meet you in person for the first time? Will you have a vibrant, driven and excited attitude? All these areas are currencies to demonstrate your value.

### 6. Be optimistic towards endless possibilities

'Optimistic towards a few possibilities' really doesn't have the same ring to it does it? That's because you've limited yourself before you've even tried. And deep down you know that if you don't try, you'll never know the true outcome. Deep down, the pain of remaining the same is greater than the pain of changing.

**Going back to your plan of attack, your approach must be in context.**

I don't think that in the history of humankind, any person has woken up and immediately thought "I really, really hope a whole bunch of emerging designers send me a generic email asking me a long list of questions which demand hours and hours of my time. Please, please, please grant me this one wish."

You need to think about what state the prospective mentor is likely to be in when receiving your communication. They're usually busy.

After asking yourself "Is online or in person the best way to contact them?", confirm your instincts with research.

The obvious starting point is to contact them where they are most active in the channel which would be easiest for them to receive your message. Twitter is great if they use it daily; however, some of your prospects don't even have an account. In which case, email or LinkedIn would be better.

A reminder that building rapport takes time, play the long-game and give them value.

As mentioned in the examples in this chapter, starting a conversation on how you've used their publicly available advice then shared it with others will give you a much higher response rate.

Why? It's because you're continuing a conversation they started. This shows that you're being real, authentic and respectful. This is expanded in the next step for you.

**Far too many people play the short game, expecting a quick win.**

# 75%

**YOU'RE CRUSHING IT!
YOU'VE COMPLETED 75%
LET'S TAKE THIS HOME!**

*Estimated section reading time: 15 minutes / completion time: ongoing*

# STEP 10: DON'T ASK FOR MENTORSHIP, ASK FOR ADVICE

**This step positions your first impression in an extremely relevant and memorable way. Asking for advice is the seed to growing a single interaction into an official mentorship relationship.**

The intention is to cut the guesswork, see the blind spots and succeed faster. We know this. That means the official 'labelling' of the mentorship relationship is secondary to the information mentors provide. If the mentorship is made official, that's helpful but not mandatory.

Try not to get distracted by formalities. Rather, stay focused on what it is you need to learn.

The next step talks about the parameters of the mentorship relationship in detail. We'll dive into that after this.

You've already identified your desired outcomes, and actions to meet them. Now we pinpoint what you're actually going to say.

## YOU MISS 100% OF THE SHOTS YOU DON'T TAKE. – WAYNE GRETZKY

Get over your fear of rejection. It does not give you anything but closed doors.

Your communication must be packaged with vibrations of effort, enthusiasm and excitement. Let prospective mentors feel this from you. Before you ask for advice, set foundations with those currencies. At this point, you would have already executed the majority of the action plan in your strategy.

**Before you ask for advice, as a minimum, make sure you've at least done the following (if applicable):**

- re-tweeted two or three of their tweets within one week, for four weeks
- liked two or three of their tweets and/or Instagram posts within one week, for four weeks
- reposted one of their Instagram posts while tagging them, with a comment on how it's inspired you or positively affected you, once a fortnight, for a month
- shared on Facebook one of their content pieces with a shout out or tagging of them (e.g. "To all my fellow designer friends, I'm sure you'll enjoy this article by <prospective mentor name>"), once a fortnight, for a month
- contributed to the conversation with a comment on two or three of their content pieces (this could be on one of their Instagram posts or stories, blog posts or videos) within one week, for four weeks.

# APPROACHES YOU CAN TWEAK AND TRY

Below are templates you can use as a base. Each requires adjusting to make it relevant to you and your prospective mentor. Deliver and execute the message in the channel in which they are most active.

This may be a direct Instagram message over Twitter, it may be a LinkedIn message over email, or it may be a Facebook messenger text over a private Snapchat message. You be the judge, based on your research. It could be the other way around. Or, it could be a face-to-face encounter at an upcoming event.

# SCRIPT 1: 'THE RESEARCHER'

*"Last month I purchased your book and online courses. I put into practice your advice and this was the result… <expand>. Would you have any suggestions for my next step?"*

Mentors love hearing constructive feedback. Let them know that you've consumed, then applied their content and the results that followed.

If you had the outcome you were after, great! If you didn't, that's fine too. In fact, it could work in your favour. There's an element of responsibility which your prospective mentor won't be able to easily ignore. They wouldn't risk damaging their credibility and authenticity after you've followed their publicly available advice. Instead, a high inclination to help you get unstuck would be why you should expect a speedy response.

Once they respond, allow this dialogue to play out naturally.

## SCRIPT 2: 'THE OBSERVER'

*"I recently watched/read/heard your interview on <source/website/podcast>. Looking back at <situation>, what would you do differently? It's similar to what I'm struggling with at the moment."*

The more your prospective mentors can see themselves in you, the more they'll be able to empathise with your situation. There's not much convincing to have them help you, because they understand the same difficulties. They've been there.

In this script, you're leveraging their nostalgia with your current challenges.

## SCRIPT 3: 'THE MEDITATOR'

*"I've recently spent some time goal setting. One main area I've identified that I need to improve on is <name goal>. It's an area that I feel you have demonstrated excellent results in. If it's not too much trouble, I would absolutely love any advice you have on this."*

A mentor can only help you if you're clear on what you need help with. This script demonstrates your self-awareness and initiative. It's framed with a great deal of respect. Between the lines, you're letting them know that you look up to them and that you've done your research.

## INITIATIVE IS YOUR RESPONSIBILITY

Mentors are usually not actively looking for you. They are, however, open and willing to mentor those who look for them. Proactivity and initiative are in rare supply. By tapping into this more, you'll turn heads.

Mentor or not, it's human nature to feel the need to help others. Whether we act on that need is another story. But the need exists because it's one way to exercise what we all seek: contribution and significance.

Those who have identified where they are right now, where they want to be, and what they need to improve on to get there, will be taken more seriously.

# WHAT TO DO IF YOU GET A 'NO'

If you get a "No" or "Sorry, I don't have time to help you at the moment" then ask for an email introduction to people in their network or circle of peers.

*"I appreciate your consideration <First Name>, thank you very much for your time. Would you by any chance have anyone within your network who could shed light on this area? Someone you could perhaps recommend and introduce me to via email? I think that would be invaluable to my <personal/professional/physical> development."*

A friend of mine said something similar in the early days of his career but added "I really want to learn from the best". Unknowingly, he used a 'Jedi mind trick'! His prospective mentor did a 180, retracted the rejection, and said "Well, there isn't really anyone else who can teach you at this level … it's okay, actually, I'll help you".

# END OF STEP 10 CHECKLIST

☐ I've consumed and digested a substantial amount of information from my prospective mentors and feel confident about their expertise, interests and tone of voice.

☐ I've re-tweeted, liked, reposted, shared, tagged and commented on their content pieces as suggested.

☐ I've chosen one of the three scripts that is most applicable to my situation and adjusted it to make it relevant to me and my prospective mentor.

☐ I've selected the channel my prospective mentor uses most and sent the message.

# KNOCK BACK A GLASS OF WATER

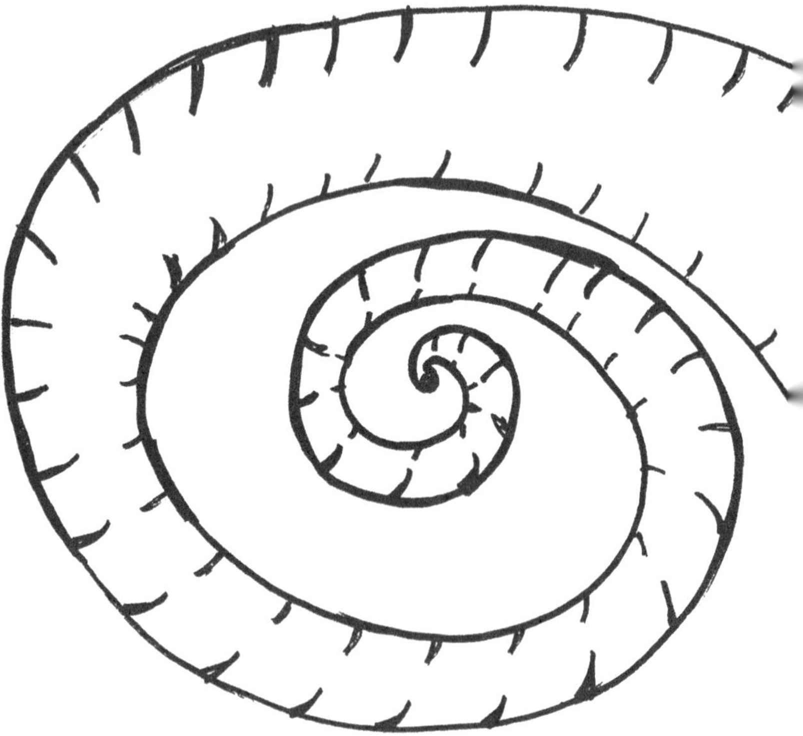

# GETTING A MENTOR WOULD MEAN FINDING NEW BEGINNINGS.

— POONAM HASSIJA,
UI DESIGNER,
@POONAMHASSIJA

*Estimated section reading time: 15 minutes / completion time: variable*

# STEP 11: SET PARAMETERS

**In this step, you attempt to find an arrangement that gives you common ground with your prospective mentor. The goal is to set mutually agreed targets to maximise productivity and ensure progress.**

At this point, you would have built enough rapport and comfort to initiate a mentor relationship. Remember, you're not demanding an official 'be my mentor' label. An element is certainly hinted but it must never be forced. Instead, you're proposing an agreed time to get together, at a certain length and at a certain frequency.

## Here's a template email or direct message approach I suggest:

(If you decide to email, I recommend the subject line: Opportunity)

*Hi <First Name>,*

*I really appreciate the guidance and advice you've generously helped me with. The last few <weeks/months> have been invaluable. Is there any way we can get together in a more consistent and frequent arrangement?*

*I know your time is precious, so am more than happy to be led by your availability in any capacity, online or offline. It certainly leans towards a mentorship style structure; however, I know the term 'mentor' can sometimes imply a commitment level outside what one can accommodate for. There is no obligation or pressure here, only an invitation. Our mutually agreed get togethers could be as little as 15 minutes on a Skype call, once every four weeks for a few months.*

*The goals I'd like to achieve in the space of <personal/professional/physical> development have been paved at a high standard by your example. I'm sure you* *would hold me accountable, which is what I feel is lacking within my current network.*

*In exchange, you can expect me to execute with open-mindedness, excitement and tenacity. It'd be an honour and I hope to do justice to any further knowledge you share with me.*

*Thank you and I look forward to hearing from you soon,*

*<Your First Name>*

**The script I've provided here is a guide. The more personalised it is as a continual dialogue from your past interactions, the more impactful this message will be.**

Tweak it if there's a clear opportunity to make it stronger. But I advise that you don't make it too lengthy. Keeping it short, relevant and of substance is vital to getting a 'yes' response. Avoid waffling or 'filler text'.

Wait for a response. If you don't get one after seven days, send a follow-up email. This is because for this type of message, in my opinion, three days isn't a huge amount of time for them to respond. They may be occupied on large projects. They may be away on business or leisure. They may just need some time to think about your invitation.

**Here's a follow-up email I suggest:**

*Hi <First Name>*

*Hoping you're having a wonderful week.*

*I'm following up to see if you had a chance to look over my last email?*

*I really appreciate your time and am grateful for your consideration.*

*Cheers,*

*<Your First Name>*

If there's still no response three full weeks after sending the first follow-up email, send one last follow-up email. Using the previous example provided, adjust it to include and specify the date when you sent the initial email regarding your invitation (which you would have sent four weeks earlier). And instead of using the words "following up" change it to "touching base". If they don't respond, it's okay. What's important is that you tried. What you must continue to do is engage with them on social media and interact with their online content. You'll still be able to learn a lot from them while simultaneously staying top of mind, being on their radar.

If they respond with a "No, I'm too busy at the moment", similar to my suggestion towards the end of step 10, ask for a referral or email introduction to one of their peers who may be able to help.

# WHAT TO DO IF THEY AGREE TO SOME TYPE OF ARRANGEMENT

There are four types of structures which can work comfortably for both you and your mentor. Your mentor will have more influence in which of the four will be chosen. It's better to assume that they have limited time to engage in mentoring sessions, rather than the other way around. The ball will naturally be in their court since you are the one asking for help. Knowing this, it's important to be as flexible as possible to whatever arrangement they can offer you.

In any case, choosing an arrangement serves two main purposes. One is to define expectations for both of you. The second is to manage the arrangement based on an agreed framework.

**Here are your four arrangement options.**

## INFORMAL, SHORT-TERM

Casual, relaxed and sometimes spontaneous. This could be a mentor relationship that lasts as little as two or three conversations over a few months, with no set order of outcomes. Each conversation length may vary. One may be 15 minutes, the next may be 90 minutes. There's an understanding of what you're specifically looking for in terms of guidance, advice and insights; however, it's not strict or highly organised about how this comes about. This arrangement is laid-back and flexible, with room to move.

Although, it does not dismiss the requirement of having a high level of commitment from both of you.

## INFORMAL, LONG-TERM

Identical to the informal nature and tone mentioned previously, this arrangement is relaxed, laid-back and unofficial. The only difference is that it's long-term, which means that it can be a relationship with interactions from a six-month timeframe to a ten-year timeframe. Because this is long-term, the frequency of engagements may be more widespread. You may have two get-togethers in one month and then none for the following two or three months. You'll know when this arrangement is the right fit because your mentor will gravitate towards this based on his or her schedule. The only thing I would advise is that you confirm that this is indeed the arrangement most convenient to them. So ask the question to ensure you're both on the same page.

## FORMAL, SHORT-TERM

Official, precise and firmly organised. Similar to the explanation of what short-term implies mentioned previously, this may only be two or three conversations over a few months. The big difference is that it is highly structured. For instance, a common arrangement would be to meet your mentor at 6:30 pm in their office on a Wednesday night, once every fortnight or once every month. The meeting would go for an hour. You'll need to be prepared with the top three itemised goals you're targeting. Or at least, what a successful outcome would look like and feel like in the area of personal, professional or physical development you seek. You'll need to take notes, listen attentively and expect to have some type of homework. Attempt to complete what is asked of you as well as possible before your next session together.

## FORMAL, LONG-TERM

Following on from the formal nature and tone mentioned previously, this arrangement is highly structured and firmly organised. The only difference is that it's long-term. So you can expect scheduled sessions that are regular and consistent over a six-month period, and possibly all the way up to ten years, depending on how the relationship develops. One hour a month over a face-to-face session or a Skype/Google Hangout call for six to nine months would be close to perfect. If I had to choose a preference from one of the four arrangements, I would choose this one, based on effectiveness alone.

**If your prospective mentor declines your invitation, use the suggested response at the end of the previous step (step 10) on 'what to do if you get a no'.**

As a mentee, you must review your goals. Make sure your mentor knows what to expect from you.

As a mentor, he or she must help set up a system to measure achievement.

Don't abuse the time and the opportunity with a mentor or prospective mentor. Fit your questions to the format and the bandwidth.

# END OF STEP 11 CHECKLIST

☐ I've reached a point where my prospective mentor has replied and engaged with me in dialogue numerous times over the course of one or two months (at least).

☐ I'm confident that there is adequate rapport and comfort between my prospective mentor and me.

☐ I've used the template email suggested as a foundation to personalise my message to my prospective mentor.

☐ I sent the message as an email or direct message (via the social media platform they use most).

☐ I understand when and how to follow up if they don't respond after seven days.

☐ In the event that my prospective mentor agrees to an arrangement, I take the initiative to suggest one of the four options that I feel would suit them best.

☐ The parameters, expectations and outcome objectives are mutually agreed upon and clear for both my mentor and me.

☐ In the event my prospective mentor declines, I respond based on the advice at the end of step 10; 'what to do if you get a no'.

—

**WE DON'T RISE TO THE LEVEL OF OUR EXPECTATIONS, WE FALL TO THE LEVEL OF OUR TRAINING.**

— ARCHILOCHUS

—

*Estimated section reading time: 15 minutes / completion time: ongoing*

# STEP 12: STAY IN TOUCH AND FOLLOW UP

**This is the final step. Then there are three consideration points to keep in mind that follow.**

Rolling off step 11, this is ongoing. It's not a one-off. Nurturing your mentorship relationships and maintaining them must be continually prioritised.

Your relationship may very well be a virtual one, since your mentor could be overseas and you initially connected with them via social media, followed by email, then Skype. All this is completely fine because staying in touch happens digitally anyway. Even if you were to plan for a face-to-face meeting, communication via the airwaves or the 'cybersphere' happens first. This is no different to staying in touch with good friends who either have busy lifestyles or who live in far places.

**Consider the following:**

## WHEN DO YOU STAY IN TOUCH?

- two or three times a year
- special occasions (e.g. their birthday, Christmas, New Year's Eve, Easter)
- national or international holidays.

## WHY DO YOU STAY IN TOUCH?

- to say hello
- to greet them
- to wish them well
- to ask them how they are
- to update them on how you are (including progress).

# HOW DO YOU STAY IN TOUCH?

- text messages
- private messages via social media (including LinkedIn and Facebook messages)
- emails
- Skype calls, Google Hangouts or phone calls.

Here are some things I have said in the past to one of my mentors, Ian, to keep in touch:

*"Hi Ian, hoping this finds you well and that you're having a wonderful year so far. I just wanted to wish you a Happy Easter! Cheers, Ram"*

*"Hi Ian, I wanted to wish you and your family a very Merry Christmas and a Happy New Year! Any plans for the holidays? Cheers, Ram"*

*"Hi Ian, I just <stumbled across/ran into> <person/place/thing> and was reminded of you. How's your <month/season/year> been?"*

# THREE POWER TIPS

1. Be guided by what comes naturally to the dynamic of both of your personalities.

2. Initiate the two or three greetings a year but don't annoy.

3. Be mindful and respectful of their time. They do not owe you anything, and a reply of any kind is a privilege not a right. Always stay grounded by the bigger picture. Most prospective mentors do want to help others and have good intentions; however, they too have multiple responsibilities, commitments and challenges.

# END OF STEP 12 CHECKLIST

☐ I completely understand that quality relationships require frequent communication and persistence.

☐ I agree and commit to keeping in touch two or three times a year with my mentor.

☐ I know why to keep in touch.

☐ I know how to keep in touch.

**100%**

**YOU DID IT!
YOU'VE COMPLETED 100% OF THE STEPS!
I'M SO PROUD OF YOU!**

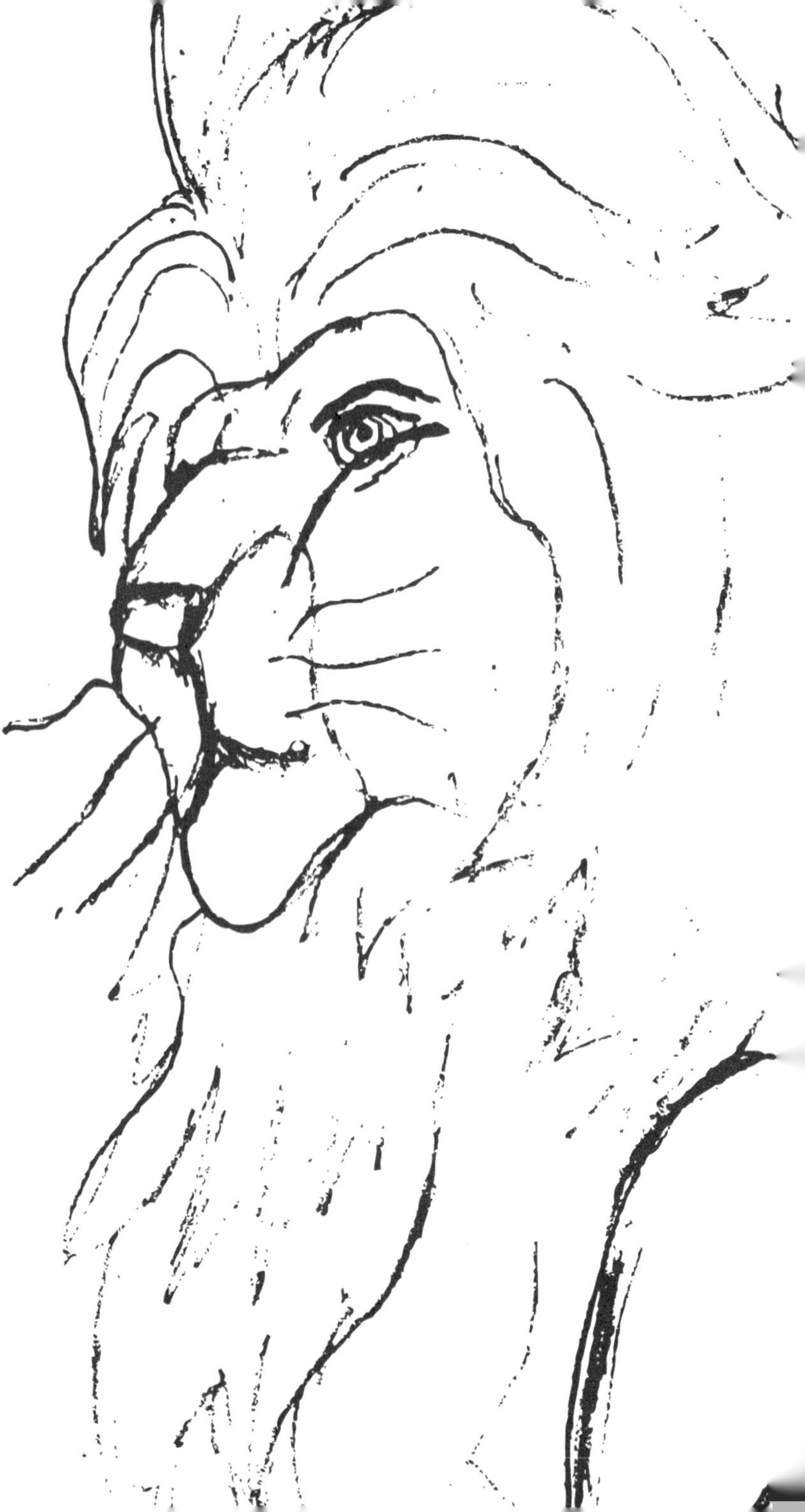

# GETTING A MENTOR WOULD INSPIRE ME TO BE TENACIOUS.

— STACY MYERS,
GRAPHIC DESIGNER,
@STACYGRAPHICDESIGNS

*Estimated chapter reading time: 20 minutes*

# THREE POINTS TO KEEP IN MIND

## 1. WHAT YOU AS A MENTEE SHOULD LOOK FOR IN A MENTOR

**Whether you intend to be part of an informal or formal mentoring relationship, some vital qualities to seek in a mentor are:**

- they are available and accessible
- they have the energy and ability to support you
- they possess a strong professional network
- they are well respected by their peers
- they have proven experience in the area you have identified for development
- they are an excellent listener
- they are trustworthy, non-judgmental and ethical

- they have a genuine interest in helping you develop personally and professionally
- they assist by providing opportunities
- they are not closed-minded and don't push their own views on you
- they are not after their own self-praise and satisfaction
- they have prior mentoring experience.

The most outstanding mentors are the ones who pour into you truths about your greatness that may not be what you're ready to hear. But they are necessary.

**This could include speaking truths and affirmations such as:**

- You will succeed.
- You will have an impact on millions.
- You will make millions.
- You will serve others in a big way.
- You will have great things happen to you.

Truths that you may not have believed in before. Unfamiliar thoughts that will slowly but surely become familiar. I had truths told to me that I didn't believe at the time. They were unfamiliar to me. However, they were reaffirmed regularly. Eventually, they became familiar.

## 2. WHAT MENTORS LOOK FOR IN MENTEES

Sadly, many people do a terrible job of attempting to find a mentor. They come across as desperate, awkward and irritating. But fear not, because successful people love helping others who take action.

Now, this may be a bit harsh, but many people need to stop being so lazy. Expect to be ignored if you are emailing questions to potential mentors that are too general or too broad. Expect to be ignored if you request them to review your portfolio as if they are sitting there counting sheep and waiting for you to contact them (I say this because I get these a lot!).

If you want a mentor, study, do your homework and stop writing generic emails. Have a real conversation.

You will find that when you do this and build rapport, play the long-game and provide them value as mentioned in step 9, you will get plenty of mentors in motion.

**Mentoring provides mentors with:**

- recognition
- a dose of regular youthful energy and enthusiasm
- a chance for them to be inspired
- a connection to the future pioneers of the industry
- credibility and reaffirmation of their own progress
- above all, the satisfaction of helping another human being reach their goals.

# 3. ARE YOU READY TO BE MENTORED?

Both individuals (the mentee and the mentor) help each other arrive at a common destination, and that is professional excellence.

**If you can answer yes to the following seven questions, you are ready to be mentored:**

1. Are you ready to accept full responsibility for your career goals?

2. Are you prepared to listen constructively and apply a mature attitude?

3. Do you understand that you are also expected to contribute to the relationship by sharing ideas?

4. Are you ready to accept constructive feedback and take suggestions with an open mind?

5. Despite being busy, are you ready to make a commitment to your future by communicating effectively with your mentor?

6. Are you ready to seriously put in the work?

7. Do you accept that in order to succeed you may fail and make mistakes in order to grow?

MY LAST FEW
**WORDS**

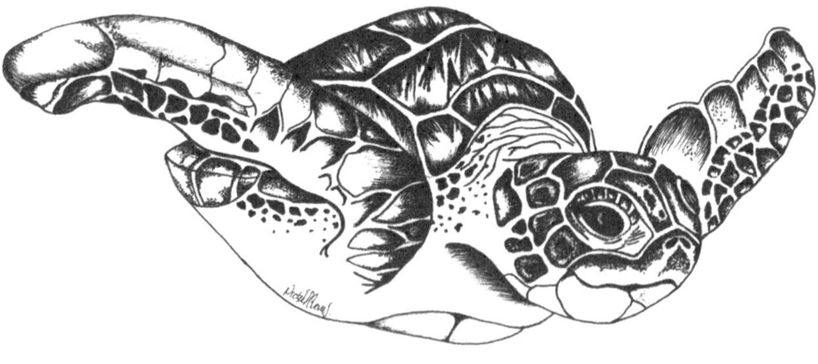

# HAVING A MENTOR HELPED ME FORM A TOUGH SHELL AS I FLOW THROUGH DESIGN AND BUSINESS CHALLENGES.

— NICTE CUEVAS,
PRINCIPAL AND CREATIVE CULTIVATOR,
NICTE CREATIVE DESIGN,
@NICTECREATIVEDESIGN

*Estimated chapter reading time: 10 minutes*

# PARTING WORDS

## SHOW UP, ESPECIALLY IN THE DARKNESS

In 2010, I went to the beautiful Yasawas islands in Fiji. At one of the islands I visited, during dinner, a 65-year-old Fijian man named Vishal invited the 40 of us present for a two-hour hike up the mountain in the middle of the island the following morning. "We have to meet here at 4 am. Who would like to join?" Vishal asked. Around 15 people raised their hands, and the joyous night continued.

I set my alarm and managed to wake up and arrive right on time at the meeting spot. There was one problem. It was pitch black and there was not a soul in sight. I had my phone to poorly light my surroundings and to check the time, which showed 4:05 am. Still, no-one.

I went through a few rabbit holes in my mind. Did I get the time wrong? The day wrong? Am I dreaming? Was this a prank?!

A few more minutes passed and I heard some footsteps. A flashlight beamed right at me. "Good morning, is it just you?" said a familiar voice. Alas! It was Vishal. "Yes" I replied, "it looks like it's just me. Are you still hiking?" "Of course", he said, "I never miss my morning hike. Come, follow me."

We started walking and a dog appeared. "Is this your dog, Vishal?" I asked. "No, but he always joins me every morning" he responded. After walking about 100 metres from the meeting spot, we arrived at the starting point of the hike; the base of the mountain. Vishal got on one knee and said, "Come, let's say a prayer for thanksgiving and protection". I closed my eyes, dropped on one knee, joined him and meditated. I felt completely at peace.

**That's him there.**

He knew where everything was. Every pathway, every tree, every rock, every piece of fruit; heck – he even knew every insect. No map could've ever replicated the intimacy with which he knew the island and the decades of experience living there.

**This is a shot of me looking out from the top of the mountain after two hours of hiking.**

Vishal was my compass for this particular mountain.

The question is, do you have the right compass for your next destination?

# LIGHT THE WAY

The last few words that I'd like to share with you are actually from my mother. As glamorous as it may seem, travelling across America for three months straight, catching planes as if they were buses was hard work and at times quite lonely.

When I was about 80% of the way through my trip, I was having a really tough time. This was triggered by Christmas Eve as it was the first time I had spent this day completely alone. Mum is one of five and Dad is one of 11 siblings. So it was a polar opposite experience to the usual family festivities. I remember ordering sushi to be delivered to my shoebox-sized San Fran apartment, while I watched a three-hour documentary about Marines.

At 11 pm my phone buzzed. It was a text from my mother, sending me a dose of her encouragement. Naturally, mothers know best and even when we plaster on a permanent brave exterior they advise us nonetheless.

> Hey Rammy, Merry Christmas. Keep painting the world with your colours and remember where you came from. Love, Mum, Dad, Ryan and Raisa

She didn't even ask how I was?! But in standard Yoda-like fashion, she didn't need to.

When I returned back to Sydney, the first thing Mum said was "How does it feel to climb up that mountain?" I smiled, and she went on to say "Make sure you come back down and share with everyone what you found".

So, I invite you to climb and conquer those mountains in and around your line of sight. Because it's the job of a designer to see things that others may not. To dive into worlds that many can't even begin to imagine. To bring back souvenirs from those places and extract what is truly important and necessary.

Like Vishal, once you've conquered that mountain, you too can light the way for others who are lost, stuck or hopeless.

It won't be a walk in the park, there will be struggles. But take comfort in knowing that it gets painfully difficult right before you succeed. Rest easy knowing that you now have the tools, steps and ability to find many more mentors from here on out.

Keep exploring, keep questioning, keep experimenting and allow yourself to be completely immersed in creativity. Because you'll find out, if you haven't already, that the entire lifestyle is a vehicle for pioneering experiences of great value.

# BE
# GIANT

# ACKNOWLEDGEMENTS

As my second published book, it's important that I acknowledge key individuals and specific groups of people who contributed to making this possible.

**God:** Thank you for driving me to the most beautiful places when I surrendered the keys.

**The Giant Thinkers community:** If it weren't for your feedback and engagement, this book would truthfully not exist. Hundreds of you have been knocking at the door of my inbox asking for help finding a mentor. Thank you for trusting in me to deliver this information to you. And thank you for inviting me into your world.

**My family:** My parents Luningning and Romulo, my brother Ryan, my sister Raisa, my grandmother Lola Carol, my partner Vivian and my guiding light Ate Salve. Thank you for being my safe haven; a place where I can always find rest whenever I'm broken and defeated. I love you with all my heart and soul.

**Illustration submissions:** Krishia Catabay, Ambrosia Sullivan, Vivian Tham, Becka Lukens, Nesibe Kaya, Ashley Sperry, José Hernández Trujillo, Yin Duan,

Poonam Hassija, Stacy Myers and Nicte Cuevas. Your drawings and reflections are a representation of what the world needs more of: authenticity, vulnerability and generosity. Thank you so much for accepting the invitation to be part of this book. I have no doubt that you will all connect with the hearts and minds of everyone who turns to your pages. Beyond that, I wish you continued fulfilment and purpose.

**My industry peers and friends:** Chase Jarvis, Matt Eastwood, Ben Fullerton, Kevin Lee, Nelson Kunkel, Chris Maclean, Vanessa Van Edwards, JP Stallard, Jules Marcoux, Jacob Cass, Daniel Flynn, Andrew Hoyne, Declan Mimnagh, Danling Xiao, Robyn Wakefield, Ric Grefé, Ted Leonhardt, Ben Abstacker, Nathan Johnson, David 'Meggs' Hooke, Lauren Currie, Monika Zands, Susan B Zimmerman, Janna DeVylder, Steve Baty, Iain Barker, Simone Blakers, Gary Smith and Ian Wingrove. The feedback and support from experts of your calibre means the world to me. It's been overwhelming to receive personal testimonials from many of you, and powerful insights from all of you, in my attempt to take this book to a world-class level. A level that aims to help everyone (not just designers), live more meaningful and purposeful lives. Know that I'm deeply humbled beyond these words and am incredibly grateful for your friendship.

**My brothers from other mothers:** Jason Seblain, Matthew Prain, Andres Pareja, Scott Stephenson, Michael Garganera, Mel Bteddini, Tunny Grattidge, Sone Lovan and Michael Schepis. Sometimes random strangers catch me eerily smiling. Little do they know of the source of my amusement as I think about the unfairly high standard of best mates I have. I love you boys. Thank you for each quality encounter. They're rare and cherished treasures.

**AIGA.org and CreativeLive.com:** Thank you for giving me the opportunity to partner and collaborate with both of your organisations over the years. To be associated with two of the most influential giants of the design and creative industry in today's generation makes my heart sing. I look forward to adding continual value to those we're able to serve.

# RECOMMENDED RESOURCES

**GiantThinkers.com**

This is my blog and podcast. It's an online resource where you'll find expert advice for emerging designers to be employed.

**Getajobasadesigner.com**

This is where you can grab my first book; *How to get a job as a designer, guaranteed.* It's been described as the most effective step-by-step guide for design students and graduates.

**Shouldyoubeadesigner.com**

I created the world's first online tool that helps aspiring designers decide whether they should pursue the path of design by answering a series of questions. The tool assesses, interprets then recommends options based on the information provided by the user and comprehensive qualitative data.

## GiantThinkers.com/CreativeLive

Here you'll find the world's largest live streaming education website; CreativeLive. Take free live online classes taught by the world's most inspiring instructors. Feel free to take a look at my classes titled *Create A Knockout Design Portfolio* and *Get The Design Job You Want.*

## AIGA.org

AIGA brings design to the world, and the world to designers. As the profession's oldest and largest professional membership organization for design with 70 chapters and more than 25,000 members – AIGA advance design as a professional craft, strategic advantage, and vital cultural force.

## Freshbooks.com/Giant

This is the #1 cloud-based accounting software for small businesses. It's especially useful if you're a freelancer. Tina Roth-Eisenberg, Founder of CreativeMornings, aka Swiss Miss, said "it saves me a huge amount of time". Forbes said it is "Incredibly user friendly". What I like most is that you can easily send invoices, track time, manage expenses, and get paid online.

**SocialElevated.com**

Meet Utah's leading video content creation service for small businesses, influencers and entrepreneurs who struggle to visually articulate meaningful stories to their audience. I use them when I'm on tour during events in the United States. They're an incredibly talented team, who are humble and love what they do.

**GiantThinkers.com/FiveMinuteJournal**

Here you'll find The Five Minute Journal, which is truly the simplest thing you can do to start your day happy. Think of it as your secret weapon to focus on the good in your life, become more mindful, and live with intention. With a simple structured format based on positive psychology research, you will start and end each day with gratitude. I absolutely love it.

**JustCreative.com**

This is the design studio website and graphic design blog of award-winning designer, good friend and industry peer Jacob Cass. His past clients include the likes of Jerry Seinfeld, Disney and Nintendo, among hundreds more. His website offers tons of resources, articles, tutorials and assets that will make you feel like you have stumbled on a gold mine.

# LET'S STAY CONNECTED
## @THEGIANTTHINKER

Please connect with me wherever you hang out on social media via my handle **@TheGiantThinker** and say hello. I'd love to hear from you and continue the conversation.

Plus, if you'd like to make a booking for a one-on-one Skype consultation, I invite you to visit **GiantThinkers.com/BookMe.**

# WANT TO HELP OTHERS FIND THEIR WAY?

If you genuinely feel this book is valuable for others in your shoes or perhaps someone similar to your younger self, an Amazon review would truly assist in reaching them. It's 60 seconds that would go a long way in helping emerging and established designers who are lost in the dark and deeply searching for guidance.

Please visit **GiantThinkers.com/MentorReview.**

That link will take you right through to the Amazon page. Let me know if you do, as I'd love to personally thank you and hear your thoughts on how it's helped you on your journey.

# INDEX

accountability 51–52, 54

advice, asking for 132–40
    template for 135–37

affirmations 165–66

Archilochus 155

barriers see obstacles

Castillo, Ram 15, 20, 23, 76, 89
    employment history of 26–30

Catabay, Krishia 4, 5

coaches 47–48

connections, lack of 93

creativity 178

Cuevas, Nicte 170, 171

D'Amato, Constantine 'Cus' 31
    design 34–35, 80
    design credibility 111

showing enthusiasm for 112–13, 127–28

designers 3, 177

Duan, Yin 120, 121

enthusiasm 112–13, 127–28, 133, 172–75

fear 92, 105, 133

Ferriss, Tim 98

Flynn, Pat 98

Ford, Henry 105

goals 22, 70–77
    being specific about 71–75
    and giving up 80
    matching mentors to 104–07
    obstacles to achieving 86–88
    overcoming obstacles 90–95
    personal 73
    physical 74
    primary 74–75, 81, 94, 106, 118
    professional 73
    timeframes for 74–75
    why you want to achieve them 79–82

Godin, Seth 105

gratitude 124–25

Gretzky, Wayne 133

Hassija, Poonam 142, 143

Hooke, David 'Meggs' 46

initiative, taking 126–27

introductions, asking for 138, 148
    template for 138

Kaya, Nesibe 84, 85

keeping in touch see staying in touch

knowledge, lack of 93

learning, continuous 125–26

lessons from book 1

lighting the way 176–78

LinkedIn profiles 111, 128

Lukens, Becka 64, 65

mentees
- attitudes of 122–30, 137–38, 167–68
- three pillars of 18, 19
- what mentors look for in 166–67
- what they are 18–19
- what they give to mentors 122–30, 166–67

mentors
- and coaches 47–48
- importance of 3, 6–9, 24, 43–45
- listing the best people 97–100
- matching mentors to goals 104–07
- purpose of 43
- qualities of 164–66
- setting parameters with 144–54
- strategy to reach them 110–19, 128–29
- three pillars of 16, 17
- three power tips for connecting with 117
- types of 71
- what they are 16–17, 47
- what they get in return 48, 122–30, 166–67
- what to look for in 164–66
- who they are 97–100
- why we crave them 22–25
- Wingrove, Ian 34–39

mentorship 42
- arrangements for 148–52
- barriers to 10–12
- formal 132–40, 150–52
- informal 132–40, 149–50
- setting parameters for 144–54
- what it is 21–25

mistakes 43

money, lack of 92

Myers, Stacy 162, 163

obstacles 86–88
- common obstacles 91–93
- overcoming obstacles 90–95

optimism 128

Partridge, Dale 98

patience, importance of 38–39

persistence, importance of 35–37, 93

personal analysis 58–63

planning, importance of 33, 127

portfolios 111

practice, importance of 45

professional development 112–13

promise letters 51–55

    personal promise letter template 52–53

rapport building 11, 33, 113, 115–19, 128–29, 166–67

rejection 133

    dealing with 138–39, 148, 152

resources 183–85

resumes 111

Robbins, Anthony 98, 105, 127

Rogers, Fred 49

self-confidence 92

showing up, importance of 172–75

side steps, importance of 26–30

Smith, Gary 66–67

social media engagement 115–17, 129, 134

Sperry, Ashley 102, 103

staying in touch 38–39, 156–60

    power tips for 159

    template for 158

    when, why and how 157–58

strategy 110–19, 127

success 45

Sullivan, Ambrosia 40, 41

templates

    asking for advice 135–37

    asking for introductions 138

    follow-up emails 147

    personal promise letter 52–53

    setting mentoring parameters 145–46

    staying in touch 158

Tham, Vivian 56, 57

time poverty 91

Trujillo, José Hernández 108, 109

Vaynerchuk, Gary 98

Vishal 172–75, 178

what you are 67–69

what you want 70–77; see also goals

who the book is for 2–3, 10–12

who you are 58–63

    questions to find out who you are 60–62

work experience, importance of 26–30

Wilson, EO 13

Wingrove, Ian 34–39